Nin

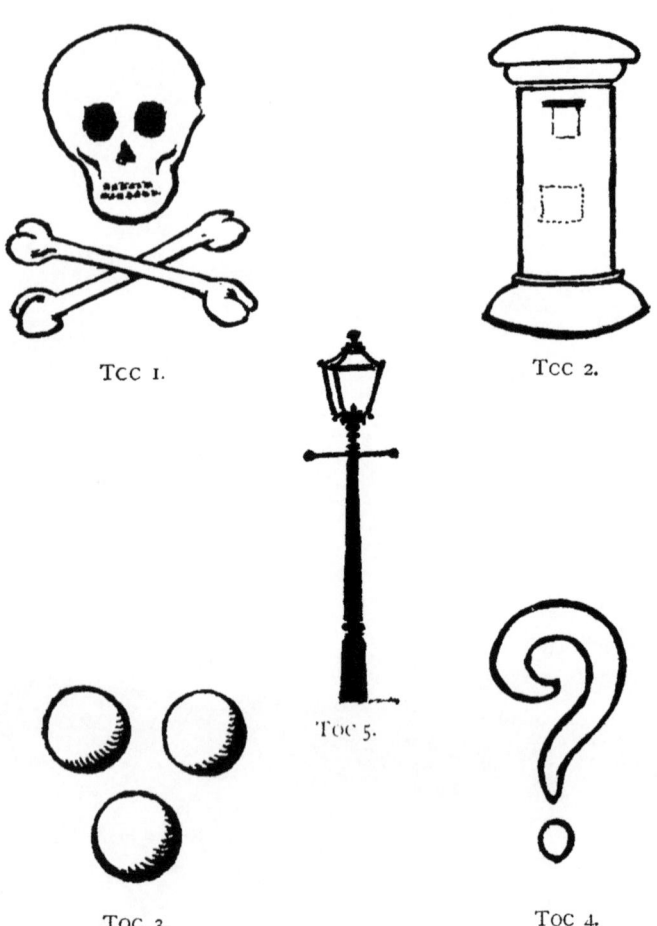

THE BATTERY SIGNS.

[THE BRIGADE SIGN IS ON THE COVER.]

NINE DAYS

Adventures of a Heavy Artillery Brigade
of the Third Army during the
German Offensive of
March 21—29
1918

BY

ARTHUR F. BEHREND
(late Captain and Adjutant, 90th Brigade R.G.A.)

(SECOND EDITION)

The Naval & Military Press Ltd

Reproduced by kind permission of the Central Library,
Royal Military Academy, Sandhurst

Published by
The Naval & Military Press Ltd
Unit 10 Ridgewood Industrial Park,
Uckfield, East Sussex,
TN22 5QE England
Tel: +44 (0) 1825 749494
Fax: +44 (0) 1825 765701
www.naval-military-press.com
www.military-genealogy.com
www.militarymaproom.com

Printed and bound in Great Britain by
CPI Antony Rowe, Chippenham and Eastbourne

In reprinting in facsimile from the original, any imperfections are inevitably reproduced and the quality may fall short of modern type and cartographic standards.

TO THOSE WHO FELL

Contents

	PAGE
APOLOGY	vii
EARLY HISTORY OF THE BRIGADE	ix
FOREWORD	xii
NINE DAYS	1
AGLIONBY'S ACCOUNT	80
FINAL HISTORY OF THE BRIGADE	92
APPENDIX:—	
How Toc 1 Lost a Piece at Miraumont Bridge	95
From Enemy Sources	98
From British Sources	100
Histories of the Batteries	101
An Unkind Story	113
Roll of Officers and Warrant Officers	114

Illustrations

DRAWINGS.

THE BRIGADE SIGN (*The Early Bird*) - -	*Cover design*
THE BATTERY SIGNS - - - - -	*Frontispiece*
ALLEGORY - - - - - - -	*To face p.* 94

PHOTOGRAPHS.

To face page

THE COLONEL - - - - - - -	ix
THE ADJUTANT AND GRAHAM - - - - -	9
TOC 1 LOADING - - - - - - -	12
TOC 5 ON THE MOVE - - - - - -	29
TOC 4 PULLING OUT - - - - - -	36
"GILLY": HATCH AND GRAINGER - - - -	38
TOC 2 READY TO FIRE - - - - -	41
TOC 3 IN ACTION - - - - - -	58
HUGH AGLIONBY - - - - - -	80
THE REMAINS OF A GERMAN DUG-OUT - - -	98
MAJOR PARGITER AND MAJOR LUSHINGTON - -	103
MILLS, WORRALL AND HARRAP - - - -	109
MAJOR CLARK AND MAJOR AUSTIN - - - -	112

MAPS.

LARGE-SCALE MAP to illustrate Fighting on March 21st and March 22nd - - - - - - - -

SMALL-SCALE MAP to illustrate Fighting from March 22nd to March 28th - - - - - - -

} *at end of book*

APOLOGY

My story was written nearly two years ago, when the events which it records were far fresher in my mind than they are to-day, —even then it could never have been satisfactorily compiled had it not been for the chance discovery, at the bottom of the Adjutant's tin box, of the file of telegrams and messages received at Brigade Headquarters on the great 21st of March, 1918.

My MS. was rescued from obscurity by the now, alas, defunct "Gunner", in whose hospitable pages parts of it appeared last spring and summer. A chance suggestion a month or two ago resulted in a circular letter going the rounds of the old Brigade: the circular was enthusiastically received—and here's the result.

My best thanks are due to the guarantors, without whose generosity nothing could have been done; to the several compilers of the Battery Histories; to H. S. G., who, not content with being a super-guarantor, undertook all the work in connection with the publicity campaign; to G. L. B. for his drawings of the maps, the signs, and the cover design; to the Keeper of Photographs, Imperial War Museum, for permission to reproduce the fine Official War Photos; and, last but not least, to anyone of the great general public who has been kind and foolish enough to buy or read a copy.

To the latter I would say:—Please remember that this is a very belated War Book written by a Gunner for all Gunners in general and for some thousand extra-special Gunners in particular. Don't be frightened of the "Pinpoints"; they are really very simple, so you musn't avoid them altogether. Just turn to the explanation on the left-hand side of the large-scale map before you start to read the story of the fighting ; you will master the system in a couple of minutes, and, once you have mastered it, you will be able to follow the speedy onrush of the Boche as easily as if you had been there yourself—and far more comfortably !

A. F. B.

January, 1921.

THE COLONEL.

A History of the Brigade

THE NINETIETH BRIGADE R.G.A.—or, as it was in those days, the 90th Heavy Artillery Group—came into being at Lydd in early 1917. Its father was Lieut.-Colonel A. H. Thorp, R.G.A., who returned from the B.E.F. for the event; its mother was Regimental-Sergeant-Major J. H. Oatley.

Between them they reared a lusty baby which, when barely old enough to walk, was taken overseas in weather cold enough to kill any but the healthiest of children.

The Railway Transport Officer at the Base told them to take it to Flanders, so to Flanders they went—to the Colonel's unspeakable disgust, for he knew the Ypres Salient so well that he never wished to see it again—and there they stayed for seven months or more.

One sunny afternoon in late June I was ordered to leave my Battery Section, which was digging-in in the middle of Ypres, and report myself at Group Headquarters in order to replace an Adjutant who was leaving. The Doc met me as I drove up and welcomed me by saying that he expected a month would be more than enough for me.

During the ghastly Third Battle of Ypres which opened on July 31st—on which day Linden, our Orderly Officer, was killed while acting as Forward Observing Officer on the Frezenberg Ridge—many different batteries passed through our hands. We moved forward into Ypres, where we passed a damp though comparatively safe couple of months in the Eastern Ramparts, alongside the dug-outs in which, a month or two later, another Heavy Artillery Group was burned alive.

The end of September found us so exhausted that, like many others, we were transferred down south to the peaceful Third Army front, where we were to rest and recuperate. We reported to the IV Corps Heavy Artillery near Bapaume and were ordered by them to proceed to Beugny, a roofless village on the Bapaume-Cambrai road, and there take over from a Group that was under orders for the Salient.

When we reached Beugny we found we had—instead of the usual crowd of guns all on top of one another within a square hundred yards—some seven miles of front and some 12 guns, of which two were so worn that they were only to open fire in the event of a grave emergency.

It really was a rest: one could with equal safety motor to Amiens to buy butter and vegetables or ride out on horseback to look for the front line. One could go and dine with one's neighbours without hearing a single shot fired: a hostile shell was an event. I remember how one of our 'planes, unable to get in touch with the Battery with which it was doing a shoot, actually landed in the Battery Position and asked the Battery Commander if all his wireless operators were on leave or merely some of them!

But the War was not won in that way and in late October we moved up towards Arras to join in a demonstration against the Hindenburg Line by Bullecourt. We silently returned to Beugny one night some three weeks later, and next day took part in the dramatic Cambrai Stunt, a show that was so nearly successful.

During the big German counter-attack we supported the gallant 56th (London) Division by firing into such places as Moeuvres and Inchy and Tadpole Copse: we like to think that it was partly due to our efforts that the Boche did not break through as he did a few miles further south at Gouzeaucourt.

About this time a much needed reform in the organisation of the Heavy Artillery came into being. Hitherto a countless succession of different Batteries had been passing through our hands, some to stay with us for a couple of weeks ; others, perhaps, for a couple of months. The confusion and unnecessary work was endless : we never really knew our Batteries, our Batteries never really knew us.

But now all this was changed. Henceforth we were to be known as a Heavy Artillery Brigade, and to us were allotted, for better or for worse, four Batteries which were to be ours for keeps until the end of the War.

And four better Batteries than Toc 1, Toc 2, Toc 3, and Toc 4,* it would have been impossible to find. I often wonder what they thought of us at first—but then our ways were certainly a little more difficult than those of some Brigades, and our telephone discipline and our system of codes were dreadfully trying until one got into them !

Soon after Christmas the whole Brigade went out of the line for a holiday at Gézaincourt, a pleasant village near Doullens, and returned to Beugny a fortnight later to take a frenzied part in the elaborate defensive preparations that were being made along the whole of the Third and Fifth Army fronts.

* Our private code-names for 95, 244, 277, and 299 Siege Batteries respectively—" Toc " being the army parlance for T, the initial letter of the Colonel's name. Toc 5 (484 Siege Battery) joined us later and was only with us for a couple of months.

.   .   .   .

Foreword

THE alleged unpreparedness of the Allies for the last German Offensive has been—and perhaps still is—a subject around which controversy has raged with considerable force.

Whatever may have been known in high places (and I have seen it stated that G.H.Q. foretold its exact day, time, and place), the fact remains that we—that is, the 90th Brigade R.G.A. and similar lowly formations—did *not* know on March 20th that the Germans were going to attack at 5 a.m. on the following morning; neither did we know that our little sector was to be the spear-head of the German effort.

Rumour, of course, had been so prolific during March that hardly a day passed without the Sergeant-Major's storekeeper or the Signal Officer or my batman being told that "the attack was going to come off in the morning but not on our front, thank goodness": or that "it should have started the day before yesterday but was put off because the wind was blowing the wrong way." And, at times, the Colonel was told the same sort of thing by people old enough and high enough to know better; but he, being a wise old bird, was not as impressionable as some of us.

It was not until the evening of March 20th that matters were clearly coming to a head, one way or the other. Just before dinner a despatch rider arrived from Corps Heavies with a hastily prepared map of the German Forward Areas in our sector.

FOREWORD

"What on earth are all those little black dots?" asked the Signal Officer jovially, looking over the Colonel's shoulder as he unrolled it.

"German guns in the open, my boy!" said the Colonel grimly, "Spotted by the Flying Corps a couple of hours ago."

And even then, as the Colonel quietly remarked during dinner, "I wonder if the wily old Boche is *really* going to attack?"

.   .   .   .   .   .

The following IV Corps Summary of March 20th, which arrived with the aforesaid map, shows how much —or how little—we knew :—

IV CORPS SUMMARY OF INFORMATION. NO. 95
20TH MARCH, 1918

ENEMY INTENTIONS. (*From Fifth Army.*)

Recently captured prisoners of various units including the 107th Division, the 44th Pursuit Flight, the 414th Trench Mortar Company and the 28th Foot Artillery Regiment were unanimous in predicting that the German offensive would commence in the next few days.

The prisoner of the 28th Foot Artillery Regiment states that the attack will be preceded by an intense bombardment, during the final two hours of which gas shells will be fired. Thereafter two hours will be allowed for the air to clear and then infantry and artillery will advance simultaneously.

HOSTILE ARTILLERY ACTIVITY.

Save for a few shells put into Demicourt to-day, hostile artillery has been very quiet.

A special reconnaissance of the area between Moeuvres and Inchy from 2.30 p.m. to 4 p.m. to-day reports a number of suspected new gun positions and material in the open, chiefly in the areas E 7 c and d,

E 8 c and E 13 b. No guns were actually seen but objects covered by tarpaulins were observed. Accurate location was difficult owing to the clouds and the large number of objects seen.

ANNEXE TO IV CORPS SUMMARY. NO. 95

Special examination of a prisoner of the 21st Bavarian Reserve Regiment, 16th Bavarian Division, captured near Bullecourt on the night of the 18th-19th March.

INTENTIONS.

Prisoner states that a huge offensive was to be carried out on the front from Rheims to Bullecourt, but the main attempts to break through would be made at both extremities.

Orders had been issued that they were to be ready by noon on the 19th, but prisoner understood that the attack had been put off, presumably owing to the weather. He had no idea how long it would be delayed.

Prisoner stated as the main opposition was expected from our airmen, a considerable concentration of hostile aircraft had been made, including Austrian and Bulgarian units.

Austrian and Bulgarian artillery was also present on the front, also a large number of Austrian Volunteer Assault Troops.

He had no knowledge about tanks.

The initial assault was to be made by specially trained Assault Divisions, but prisoner was under the impression that his Division would also take part in the attack.

Prisoner admitted that he had been examined three times but that he was careful not to give anything away.

(*From Third Army Summary.*)

Information obtained from a deserter of the 28th Reserve Infantry Regiment, 185th Division, who surrendered in our lines near Bullecourt on the night 17th-18th March, 1918.

FOREWORD

CIRCUMSTANCES OF CAPTURE.

Prisoner was on fatigue carrying duck-boards to the enemy's front line. The line was thinly held and he seized upon a favourable opportunity to desert.

Prisoner is a Pole, born in March 1898, and was called up in October 1917. He has a strong dislike for the Germans and on the 8th inst. tried to desert back to Germany. Having reported sick, he went to Douai but was refused admission to the hospital; he thereupon took a train and succeeded in reaching Louvain via Tournai and Brussels; he was, however, arrested at Louvain on the evening of the 9th inst. and sent back under escort to his regiment on the 12th.

PREPARATIONS FOR AN ATTACK.

The last few nights prisoner's company has been employed in carrying trench mortar ammunition towards the front line. The work was very heavy but the men were urged to do their utmost as the work was pressing.

TANKS.

Prisoner has never seen any tanks or heard anything about German tanks but he states that on the 15th, when on a daylight patrol, he had seen a notice board on which was written "Tank Stelle 7." All the men were much surprised. Prisoner thinks the board is placed on a track which has been prepared for tanks as he noticed that a track had been to a certain extent levelled by shell holes having been partly filled in.

GENERAL.

There is a great deal of talk about an impending offensive and a state of tension appears to exist amongst the troops. All sorts of rumours are current. The back areas are said to be full of troops of an assault division. Prisoner has no idea who this division may be.

Several dates have been mentioned for zero day, the original date having been the 12th; then the offensive was said to have been postponed to the 14th, then to the 18th.

Hindenburg, Ludendorff and the Crown Prince are said to have been in Douai on the 12th.

His Company Commander told prisoner that an offensive was imminent and the men are being continually urged to hurry work and are made to work very hard. As regards details, prisoner states that no one but Hindenburg himself knows what is really going to happen, and he can only repeat rumours.

AUSTRIAN ARTILLERY.

On the occasion whilst prisoner was on patrol and saw the " Tank " notice board, he also saw an Austrian Artillery Officer who asked his way to a battery. On the 12th in Louvain, whilst with his escort to return to Douai, prisoner saw three trains of Austrian Artillery in the railway station.

RELIABILITY.

Prisoner is a genuine deserter. He is very talkative and rather excitable but, only having joined his regiment in January, he has little military experience and therefore is not in a position to form a critical opinion of his own.

MARCH 21ST, 1918

I awoke with a tremendous start conscious of noise, incessant and musical, so intense that it seemed as if hundreds of devils were dancing in my brain. Everything seemed to be vibrating, the ground, my dug-out, my bed. What on earth was up ? By Jove ! The great Boche offensive must have begun ! It was still dark. What time was it ? Just five o'clock.

I lit a candle, seized the telephone receiver beside my bed and buzzed up the exchange.

" Any messages coming through ? " I asked.

" No, sir ! "

" Then put me through to Tusculum."

" Mr. Gardiner's speaking to them now, sir."

The door of my dug-out opened and in hurried the Colonel, clad in spectacles, pyjamas and gum boots.

" Any report from the O.P. ? " he asked.

" Gardiner's speaking to them now." Suddenly a terrific crash half lifted me out of bed. Out went the candle.

" Beside the clerks' dug-out," remarked the Colonel, peering down the road.

A wave of emotions came tumbling into my excited brain. During the past few months, despite the fact that we were barely five thousand yards from the front line, the war had seemed so remote that we might have been fifty miles away from it. No shell had fallen within a thousand yards of us ; our batteries had been living in comfort and luxury; visits to O.Ps. or trips up the line were as devoid of incident as tramps over the Yorkshire Moors.

Since the Cambrai show the whole Brigade had barely had a dozen casualties; in fact since Christmas life on the Bapaume front had been exceedingly pleasant—a succession of glorious canters across the overgrown downs to the Batteries, joy-rides to Amiens through the snowy wastes of the Somme, early morning partridge shoots over the fields around our headquarters.

All these happy memories came tumbling through my mind to be overwhelmed by this one tremendous fact—that a big shell had fallen in the roadway ten yards from my dug-out. . . .

The Colonel interrupted my train of thought. " Where are the S.O.S. orders ? " he asked.

" In Gardiner's dug-out, sir—he was on duty last night."

The Colonel hurried off. Big stuff was now falling all around us thick and fast and I wondered how much longer it would be before my shack would get a direct hit. The concussion was so intense that it was impossible to light the candle. Suddenly the door blew off its hinges. Outside dawn was slowly breaking as if anxious to soften the vivid flashes of the shells that were bursting everywhere. Volumes of dust and smoke drifted past the door blown this way and that by the fury of the storm. The fascinating smell of high explosives and ravaged earth bewildered me.

I don't know how long I lay in bed—it must have been nearly five minutes. I was trembling with excitement—or was it fear ?—and I felt powerless to move—besides, what was the use ? There was nothing to do and one might just as well be killed decently in bed instead of half naked, while struggling into one's shirt. . . . By Jove, what a tremendous barrage the Boche was putting down. All our lines must have gone during the first minute. . . . Served us right for not getting the " Bury "* finished in time. . . . If our barrages in the Salient last year were anything like this, no wonder the Boche lost the Passchendaele Ridge. . . . Lord! That one was damned near ! . . . What a stink ! Must be gas ! . . . Wonder what sort of a time the Batteries are having ? . . . And the Infantry. . . . Pretty bloody, I suppose. . . . Boche got through yet ? . . .

It is curious how rapidly the human mind accustoms itself to the most abnormal conditions. Within a few minutes—so it seemed to me—I had been living in this inferno for years and years and intense shell fire became quite the usual state of affairs. A desire for action came back to me. I got out of bed and, in the reeking semi-darkness, put on my clothes. The thought of survival hardly entered my head. Even if one was only wounded one would have a precious small chance of getting away. . . . One might be captured though, so it would be better to put on my new tunic, the one with the chevrons on it. . . .

We had often discussed what we would do when the Boche launched his big offensive ; most of us had pictured ourselves lining the sunken road with—if one were lucky—one of the dozen rifles which our Mobilisation Equipment tables allowed us.

Well, here was the reality !

I put on my belt, fastened my gas-bag at the "Alert",

* A big buried cable system that was being laid down by Corps.

crept out into the roadway and ran for Gardiner's dug-out.

"Every line has gone except the 'fool' (ground) one to Toc 6!" said the Colonel bitterly. "And, thank goodness, the Bury from Toc 6 to Tusculum is still through."

"Any news from Tusculum?" I asked.

The Colonel handed me a telephone message:—

"S.O.S. on Left Division front. All our Batteries seem to have opened out. Tusculum."

It was now about twenty past five and quite light though there was so much mist and smoke that it was hardly possible to see a hundred yards. The shelling of our headquarters seemed to be over*; in front, however, the noise was greater than ever.

The Colonel went off to his shack to dress: I heard him shouting for his shaving water. I went outside again. Things had changed almost beyond recognition. The roadway was covered with earth, stones and great lumps of turf. A dozen great shell-holes, still smoking, gaped in the middle of the road and all our beautiful telephone wires were trailing helplessly in the dirt. I climbed up on top of the roadbank and saw new shell holes everywhere, hundreds of them. A big shell passed swiftly far overhead, bound for Bapaume or Achiet-le-Grand. The smoke was clearing away; I turned to watch the Boche straffing our six-inch gun Battery (Toc 5) who were firing merrily away half-a-mile in front. Jolly good, I thought, for they had only been

* Several months later during the advance, one of our batteries found a Boche map dated March 18th, on which our headquarters were marked as a Telephone Centre. The Boche must have thought (and rightly) that twenty minutes concentrated fire would finish us off.

out a couple of months and the Boche appeared to have them taped.

While I was watching, the Sergeant-Major appeared walking smartly up the road, as spick and span as if he were going off on his weekly trip to the laundry at Albert. I noticed that he, too, had his best tunic on!

" Jenny's (one of our horses) been killed and the car's had a narrow escape, sir ! The bottom half of the garage has been blown in but the car doesn't seem to have been touched. Thompson's trying the engine now. No casualties among the men—we've been lucky! As soon as they've had breakfast I'll put them on repairing the roadway. It looks nasty, doesn't it, sir ? "

" Right-o, Sergeant-Major ! Send all the men not on duty into the mined dug-out ; there's no knowing when he'll start up again on us. Leave the horses in the stable ; they're as safe there as anywhere."

The office—a Nissen hut—was so perforated that it looked like a pepper-pot and I noticed with resentment that one big shell splinter had come in exactly where I usually sat and embedded itself deep in my table. Neither the Colonel nor I relished the idea of working there so we carried the map boards across to his shack, which at least had the protection of the road bank.

The battle situation was so obscure that for all we knew we might already be surrounded. Of what was happening in front we knew nothing. We were in touch with our immediate superiors, Corps Heavy Artillery Headquarters—known familiarly as Corps Heavies— merely by wireless ; we were out of touch with all our Batteries except Toc 6 (a detached section of 95 Siege Battery), to whom we were through by means of a ground line over a mile in length which, strange to say, kept through all day and I don't know what we would have done without it. As previously stated, Toc 6 were in touch with "Tusculum", the Brigade O.P., by means of a buried cable several feet deep.

The officer manning Tusculum said there was too much mist and smoke to see anything but that rifle fire was still incessant and Boche shell fire still very heavy, especially in Morchies—on the outskirts of which were two of our Batteries, Toc 4 and Toc 1.

Toc 6 were at the back of Vaulx; there was an Infantry Brigade Headquarters (of the 25th Division) five hundred yards in front of them so Toc 6 were told to send an officer across for news. Throughout the day the Infantry Brigade in Vaulx proved one of our most reliable sources of information but Toc 6 must have blessed us as each trip to the Infantry meant running the gauntlet through the village, which was heavily shelled from dawn to dusk.

For many weeks past elaborate orders had been issued to us almost daily telling us what our Batteries were to do when the Boche attacked. These orders, with their fresh targets and new rates of fire, became so complicated that it was almost impossible to compete with them and with their numerous additions, amendments, additions to amendments, and amendments to additions. Luckily in the end Corps Heavies took pity on us and, with a wonderful burst of energy, issued on the eve of the battle a fairly lucid five-page document which, as the Brigade-Major remarked, was positively the last word and contained all the winners.

Broadly speaking, the Artillery defence was divided into two phases, Counter-preparation and S.O.S.

Counter-preparation was intended to cramp the enemy's style as much as possible while he was massing for the attack; the targets were such things as communication trenches, support trenches or road junctions through which he was likely to go. The moment the Boche " came over the top", Batteries were to switch to their S.O.S. targets—a barrage along the middle of No Man's Land. As it had been realised that communications would probably have " gone west " by this time, more elaborate instructions had been issued telling the Batteries how to recognise the fateful moment. Judge the results of this thoroughness!

About six o'clock a wireless message arrived from Corps Heavies " You should be firing Counter-preparation." I rang up Toc 6 and asked them if they were firing Counter-preparation. No, they were firing S.O.S. as judging by the heavy rifle fire (vide para 3 (a) on page 2 of Artillery Instructions XX.), the Boche had already come across!

(As a matter of fact the Boche did not leave his trenches until 8.30 a.m. though it was afterwards reported that his pioneers were seen soon after five o'clock standing upright in our wire, cutting lanes through it with wire-cutters.)

The practical side of the defensive arrangements had not been neglected, either. Since Christmas the front line system had been enormously strengthened and a fine reserve line, known variously as the Haig Line and the Brown Line, had been dug about three thousand yards behind the front line. Unfortunately on our front the Brown Line only consisted of a single wide trench—had there been a support trench the day might have gone differently for once our Infantry were driven out of the

Brown Line there was nowhere for them to rally for a counter-attack.

The next defensive system was the Army or Red Line and ran just behind our headquarters. It was merely an old Boche trench; consequently the wire was on the wrong side and men were working feverishly on it all day. Behind the Red Line there was nothing but the wastes of the Somme, which in the end proved the most effective brake of all.

The Artillery defences were far more thorough and complete. All the Battery positions had been wired in and dozens of reserve positions and O.Ps. had been made, to cover both the Brown and the Red Lines.

Our Brigade had been responsible for the construction of at least a dozen reserve positions—one of which, to our disgust, was in the middle of our headquarters. All this had meant weeks of real hard work as six gun-pits had to be dug at each position, wooden gun platforms had to be laid (and guarded from marauders), camouflage had to be erected over each pit, command posts had to be sunk in the ground (and drained), and hundreds of rounds of " juice " dumped on each position (and counted). Even the Adjutant did his bit for, apart from indenting for all the pit-props and the elephants and the rabbit wire and the duck boards and the nine-by-three and the camouflage and the fuzes and the sand-bags and the corrugated iron and the one-inch nails and the six-inch nails, apart from organising their collection, apart from fighting with Siege Park for more lorries and more lorries and more lorries, apart from wringing huge working parties from abusive Battery Commanders, apart from imploring Corps Heavies to send up less ammunition, apart from all these things

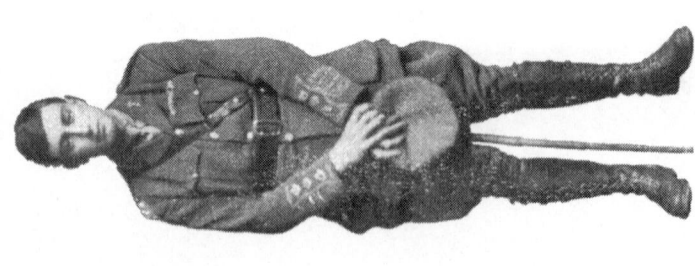

THE ADJUTANT.

GRAHAM RETURNING FROM THE INVESTITURE.

and a hundred more, he was responsible for erecting boards at each position so that inspecting generals should know, for instance, that the neat little notice board " H.A. 107 " beside that nasty wet hole covered with a sheet of corrugated iron really marked the Battery Commander's Post of Heavy Artillery Reserve Position No. 107.

Such, in a nut-shell, was the situation at seven o'clock on the morning of the twenty-first of March in the year of grace nineteen hundred and eighteen, when the Colonel and the Adjutant of the finest Heavy Artillery Brigade in the British Army sat in a shack near Beugny, in the Province of Artois, France, staring at a map-board in front of them and wondering what on earth was going to happen next (at least the Adjutant was).

The skies hummed with 'planes but, owing to the low visibility, there was little definite information from them.

Judging from the numbers of " W.P." zone calls coming down (used when hostile batteries are too numerous to pin-point), every map square behind the Boche lines was teeming with artillery and, as an R.F.C. observer afterwards remarked to me, " in addition to every gun, howitzer and trench mortar from Central Europe, the Hun must also have been using drain-pipes !"

Suddenly a Boche 'plane made a spectacular and successful attack on a kite-balloon which had risen a mile behind us. Flying very low he circled round and round it, machine-gunning away for all he was worth. Out tumbled two wretched balloonatics, their parachutes opened just as parachutes should open, the balloon burst into flames and turned into a streak of dense black smoke, whilst the Boche flew gaily away with every anti-aircraft battery within range (and several that weren't) firing wildly at him.

A few minutes later a five-nine H.Vic (High Velocity) shell came at us with a sickening scream and fell in the roadway near the garage. With one exception the men who were at work clearing up the road downed tools and scurried like rabbits for cover. The exception was a gunner named Freshwater.

A slight digression is here necessary. Gunner Freshwater was a wonderfully hard worker and a first-rate handyman but he had one peculiarity—if that be the correct word. During the year he had been with us he had never *once* been known to say a single word to anyone unless absolutely compelled to do so by desire for some essential such as leave or food or a new pair of boots. (No, he was not a Scot ; he was a Yorkshireman.) The Colonel, who never could remember names, had once hailed him with " Come here, carpenter ! " but Freshwater took not an atom of notice. The Colonel went up to him. " Didn't you hear me calling you ? " he asked. Freshwater looked at him in his queer way for nearly a quarter of a minute. " Yes," said he slowly, adding " Sir " as an afterthought, " I 'eard you all right but I'm not a carpenter ; my name is Gunner Freshwater ! " Freshwater had one additional eccentricity. When he was given a job of work to do he would work like a horse at that job of work until it was breakfast time or dinner time or tea time or bed time. But as soon as it was any of those times he would stop work suddenly, even if he were three-quarters of the way up a ladder with two heavy sandbags on his back !

Consequently when the shell fell, Gunner Freshwater carried on.

"Get under cover, Gunner Freshwater!" roared the Sergeant-Major, who was the only man from whom Freshwater would take orders.

Freshwater paused with his barrow in the middle of the road and looked round to see who was shouting. As he looked round a second shell tore over our heads and burst with a rattling report at Freshwater's very feet. When the smoke and the dust had cleared away we could see him lying dead on the road with his barrow beside him.

Then that damned gun lengthened its range; its third shot fell plumb in the middle of the Field Ambulance down at the bottom of the road. Up rose clouds of black smoke, earth, and fragments of Nissen huts. It was perhaps the most sickening sight I have ever seen and I can picture it to-day as vividly as if it had happened yesterday morning. A few figures ran helplessly hither and thither among the huts and among the scores of loaded stretchers that lay all around. It was like prodding an ant's nest with a stick, except that the ants were human beings and the nest was a Hospital. . . . The bombardment lasted over a quarter of an hour, two or three shells a minute. Sometimes the shells fell amongst the huts, sometimes amongst the stretchers. . . .

The German gunners must have shuddered had they seen the effects of their handiwork—it is, however, only fair to say that they were probably shooting at the Cambrai Road, alongside which the Field Ambulance had mistakenly been sited.

Luckily there was but little time for thinking about

such things ; at half-past ten a dusty and panting runner arrived from Toc 1 with a welcome and comforting message from Major Pargiter :—

" Still firing S.O.S. Normal rate. All O.K. here. Wireless gone west. Any fresh orders ? Nothing to be seen from Tusculum, and Brigade* had nothing except Boches massing in front of Quéant."

We had no fresh orders ; we gave the runner a drink and sent him back with the news that all was well at Toc 6 and that we knew nothing about the situation.

A few minutes later a runner arrived from Toc 2, who lived behind a desolate copse named Maricourt Wood, mid-way between Morchies and Vaulx. Toc 2 were commanded by Aglionby—Major Lushington was on leave—and his message ran :—

" Lines still down. Enemy fire persistent but slackening. Am still firing Counter-preparation. No zone calls received. Wireless aerial damaged but still in action. No wounded or stragglers have passed here."

This last sentence was a just tribute to the 25th Division. We sent the runner back to Toc 2 with orders for them to switch at once to S.O.S. targets.

The suspense was becoming unbearable. What was happening ? Was the Boche through ? Even the Colonel began to fidget ; suddenly he said to me, " Tell the Sergeant-Major to get that horse of ours buried ! "

I knew the Colonel too well to attempt to argue with him so out I went to find the Sergeant-Major who, when I told him, looked pained but said nothing. Ten minutes later I strolled down to see how they were getting on.

* An Infantry Brigade Headquarters of the 6th Division who lived in palatial dug-outs near Toc 1.

Toc 1 Loading.

Reproduced by permission of the Imperial War Museum.

The Sergeant-Major, Fulton (the Artillery Clerk) and half-a-dozen more were digging away silently. Shrapnel shells were whining over our heads and bursting with pretty white puffs over the Cambrai Road a quarter of a mile away. The sight of a First Class Warrant Officer and six men burying a horse while the Boche was thundering at our very gates appealed to my sense of humour so I took off my coat and helped them to haul poor Jenny into her grave. It always annoys me when I think of the time we wasted burying her but it must have been a horrid task for the Boche digging her up again and burying her decently, for her grave was barely eighteen inches deep !

Toc 5 provided us with the only other comic relief of the day.

As I have said before Toc 5 had only been out a couple of months and, during their first few weeks, the punctuality with which they sent in the daily peace-warfare returns left much to be desired. So it spoke volumes for the fear inspired in them by the Adjutant when about two minutes past twelve a breathless officer arrived and solemnly handed him the Noon to Noon Ammunition Return. He saluted and said,

" Major Austin told me to say he's very sorry if this is a few minutes late but under the circumstances he hopes you won't mind, sir ! "

During the last half-hour the visibility had improved greatly ; at ten minutes to twelve a telephone report from Tusculum told us that the Boche had managed to break through :—

" Enemy advancing on Lagnicourt at 11.30. Numbers of infantry and cavalry and tanks on right of Pronville."

This was straightway telephoned back to Corps Heavies (with whom we were once more in fitful communication); the latter part of the message must have caused much fluttering in the dovecots for Boche tanks were then an unknown quantity.

Next a report arrived from our furthermost Battery, Toc 3, who were in an exposed position two thousand yards in front of Morchies, just north of the Bapaume-Cambrai road. Toc 3 had sent the message by runner to Tusculum whence it had been telephoned to us. It was a great relief to hear from them though their news was alarming :—

"F.O.O. reports column of men and horses advancing over crest in front of Fungus, and down valley and left past tanks over crest. Infantry in valley to left of O.P."

Fungus (so-called because it had sprung up in a night) was a forward O.P. near Louverval, manned that day by an officer of Toc 3. The middle part of the message was meaningless but it showed that the Boche had made another breach in our line. What infantry, I wondered, looking at the map-board? Not Boche, I hoped, or Toc 3 would be soon surrounded. Barely five minutes later a second and terser message arrived from Toc 3 :—

"O.C. Battery wounded. Bengough and two O.Rs. killed."

Poor Bengough! He was an elderly subaltern: orders had reached us that very morning for him to proceed to England for duty with the Ministry of Munitions.

Mills, the Captain of Toc 3, was doing an Artillery Course at Lydd so, now that Major Sunley was wounded, the command of the Battery devolved on the subalterns and I wondered what chances they would have of getting him back to C.C.S.* He had only just been awarded an M.C. for rescuing an airman who had crashed near the front line. Messages now began to come in fast. "Dog", the code name for the Infantry Brigade near Toc 1, sent us a wire by some devious route—probably through Division :—

> "Situation does not appear satisfactory. We are still holding the reserve line D 25 a to J 2 b. Enemy batteries reported D 13 d 9.0 (*the old No Man's Land in front of Quéant*) some time back and D 26 b 7.7 (*well inside our old Front Line.*) recently AAA† Numerous Huns in Leech Avenue and Lynx Support D 26 b AAA Consider batteries and trench named in last para are your best targets. Pretty heavy fire would be appreciated."

Things were getting serious. The Boche had already been able to get his artillery across No Man's Land and into action well inside our lines. Toc 3 were certainly outflanked and might by now be surrounded: the Boche seemed to be doing extraordinarily well.

The message from "Dog" was immediately amplified by a message from Tusculum :—

> "German line now in front of wire of reserve line. Get on to area D 26 a and b."

We ordered Toc 6 to sprinkle a dozen into D 26 a and b.

At a quarter past one another appeal from "Dog" reached us timed, unfortunately, 12.25 so it was too late to help them :—

> "Enemy now in great numbers in Louverval and advancing against our intact reserve line in D 26."

* **Casualty Clearing Station.**   † AAA signifies a full-stop.

Next a badly wounded runner struggled in with a letter from Clark, the Major of Toc 4, who were on the outskirts of Morchies. This was the first message we had had from them; as we feared, they had been getting it in the neck. Timed 12 noon and covered with bloody finger marks, it ran :—

"Since my last message (*which, by the way, we had never received*) my position has been very heavily shelled and I have only been able to keep in action at intervals. I have expended 200 rounds on Counter-preparation and S.O.S., and succeeded in getting off about 25 rounds on an enemy concentration in D 26, at request of DOG. My F.O.O. (*who had been manning one of the reserve O.Ps.*) reports that the barrage at 11 a.m. was only heavy on the Left Division front (*the 25th*). My Battery is evidently under observation as directly I open fire I am engaged by about four 5.9 H.V. guns. My casualties are at present about 1 officer and 10 O.Rs. wounded and 5 O.Rs. killed."

So "Dog's" appeal had not been in vain! Well done, Toc 4!

A few minutes later another runner arrived from Toc 1 :—

"Attached is from DOG," wrote the Major. "I am engaging at their request the Hun Battery at D 13 d 9.0 with one piece and the Strand with two pieces."

The attached message :—

"Huns at 11.45 advancing down valley J 2 b and in great numbers through Louverval towards the Cambrai Road. So far as we are concerned we believe the reserve line on the 6th Division front to be intact, but to our right the enemy has got through reserve line and is advancing against Brown Line. I hear that the Hun is in Noreuil."

Things were getting worse and worse.

At 1.12 Tusculum telephoned:—

"Much hostile artillery advancing along Pronville-Lagnicourt road. Germans concentrating at J 8 b."

J 8 b was only a thousand yards from Toc 3.

Five minutes later Tusculum reported:—

"Germans advancing from J 8 b."

Heaven help Toc 3! Would we ever see them again?

Then a belated message, timed 12.50, arrived via Toc 6 from the Infantry Brigade at Vaulx:—

"Enemy reported to be digging in in front of Brown Line."

The Boche wouldn't be digging in unless they were held up; good old 25th Div!

A second note arrived from the skipper of Toc 2:—

"Wounded infantry N.C.O. (reliable) reports that we hold Brown Line. Wounded trench mortar gunner (not reliable) reports enemy in Lagnicourt. Wounded West Yorks. officer reports Boche held Travel Trench at 11.30, but the Essex were about to counter-attack. We bombed enemy half-way out of Leech Avenue."*

Our line to Toc 2 must have then been put through for a telephone message was brought in from them:—

"DIBS (*the code name for an Infantry Brigade Headquarters of the 6th Division near Lagnicourt*) report that enemy are massing in eastern outskirts of Lagnicourt and that bombardment would cause great execution AAA I have engaged and repeated to Toc 1."

Ten minutes later Tusculum reported:—

"White rocket fired from Lagnicourt and enemy visible on western outskirts."

* Compare with first message from "Dog".

So battered old Lagnicourt had gone! The white rocket must have been the signal of its capture.

The next message showed that Toc 2 were having it hot :—

"We are running short of tubes. Please give bearer 200. The Boche is in the Sunken Cross Roads where DIBS were. We have just pushed him up the hill with our barrage and he has retreated to the Cross Roads again. Infantry now up to support."

I knew the Sunken Cross Roads well; the Colonel and I had been to "liaze" with Dibs two or three mornings ago. I looked at the map and was wondering what had become of them when the telephone orderly ran in with perhaps the most dramatic message of all. Toc 6 had 'phoned it to us; it had been given to them by the Pigeon Loft near their position :—

"To 6th Division. We hold most of Bradford Reserve and Skipton Strong Point AAA All papers and plans destroyed AAA Boche are all round AAA We are manning road round Headquarters AAA Shorten artillery barrage. DIBS. (By pigeon service.)"

Well played, Dibs! We never heard of them again.
At three o'clock a wire arrived from Corps Heavies as if in answer to our unspoken thoughts :—

"No orders can be given for withdrawal of batteries at present. Batteries must hold on if possible. Any zone calls from the air should be answered if possible and also any orders from 6th Divisional Artillery."

The Colonel snorted. It was an insult to tell our Batteries to "hold on if possible"—of course they would. And of course "zone calls from the air would be answered if possible."

To us on the spot there seemed, unfortunately, no doubt that the time had come to withdraw the Heavy Artillery in our sector but we realised how difficult it was for the powers-that-be to make their decision. So many factors had to be considered—for instance the situation on the front of the flank corps, the supply of reserves, and the fact that it would soon be growing dusk. However, it was plain that every five minutes' delay would jeopardise the chances of getting our guns away.

At ten minutes past three a significant LL call (Special Opportunity Target) came down from the air :—

" 1000 Fan. C 14 d 8.0."

which, being interpreted, meant that the Boche infantry were a thousand strong in Vraucourt Copse. Toc 6 for one answered the call; the range was barely 2000 yards.

Between three and four there was a distinct lull as though both sides were licking their wounds though the noise of rifle fire grew ominously nearer and nearer. A reserve battalion of the 25th Division came up in artillery formation ; several small parties crossed the roadway beside our headquarters. They were under no illusions as to the hell which lay a couple of thousand yards in front of them and some of them looked enviously at us in our comparative safety.

At 4.25 p.m. two even more significant zone calls came down :—

" G.F. Art. S.W. C 18 b 9.7." (*Fleeting opportunity target: Artillery moving South-West along Quéant-Lagnicourt road.*)

" C 17 a 2.5 N.F." (*Battery Now Firing from just north of Lagnicourt.*)

The Boche was certainly moving his artillery forward with wonderful speed. Hurry up, Corps Heavies, or it will be too late!

The next report rushed our thoughts a mile or two further south whence news of late had been scarce :—

"4.35 p.m. Large bodies of Boche advancing up valley between Morchies and Louverval. Am engaging. Juice running short. Toc 1."

. . . . . .

Just as the suspense was becoming well nigh unbearable came the orders, welcome yet unwelcome :—

"Batteries will retire to reserve positions covering Brown Line."

"Not far enough!" growled the Colonel, "The Boche will be on top of us again before we've been in action an hour or two!"

Runners from all the Batteries except Toc 3 were standing by: we sent them off in pairs with the fateful news. Bell, of Toc 3, was manning Tusculum; we told him to try to get back to his Battery as there was still a sporting chance for them.

While the drama was unfolding I had plenty of work but now I felt that the least I could do was to go round the Batteries and see how they were getting on so I sent down to Thompson to bring up the car and told my ancient batman to pack up my kit while I was away.

Thompson appeared, as imperturbable as ever, and off we went. It was nearly dark as we slipped past our headquarters and turned into the Cambrai Road. Save for the crackle of musketry away on the left, complete and uncanny silence reigned. Beugny seemed strangely deserted. We sped on and on past the sad trees that flanked the road until we reached the cross roads at the Sugar Factory—its ruins ghostlier and grimmer than ever. We turned off towards Morchies.

Hatch, a very gallant subaltern who had won the M.C., D.C.M., and M.M., was in charge of operations at Toc 1; the Major had walked over to Vaulx to encourage Grainger, Badman and Tuck at Toc 6.

The big nine-twos were being dismantled; the barrels had already been hauled on to their transporting wagons and the "Cats" (caterpillar tractors) were standing by in noisy readiness. Thanks to their fine deep pits, Toc 1 had escaped with few casualties; everyone was hard at work and seemed very cheery and full of buck so I walked across to Toc 4, a few hundred yards away, stumbling in and out of stinking new shell holes.

Toc 4 had previously had a snug position in the middle of Morchies but a week before the attack the Army Commander had ordered all Battery positions in villages to be moved. It was a wise precaution for Morchies, always a sorry sight, now looked a mere shadow of its former self.

Toc 4 had certainly had it in the neck; their morale was noticeably lower than that of Toc 1. The ground all around their position was simply ploughed up by shell fire and the position reeked so much of Yellow Cross gas that it was a wonder they had been able to carry on at all. I saw the gun-pit which had been wrecked by a direct hit. The whole detachment, including Fisher, had been killed or wounded and cartridges and fuzes had gone up galore but, strange to say, the how. itself was only slightly damaged. Debris, human and otherwise, lay around the pit.

Toc 4 seemed glad to see me ; I told them how the other batteries of the Brigade had fared and went on my way rejoicing with half a tumbler of neat whisky inside me.

Thompson had turned the car round ; we drove back to the Sugar Factory and turned towards Cambrai. Save for a few odd Jocks and a dead mule, the road was deserted. I was wondering where the Boche was when an officer appeared in the roadway in front of us.

" Stop ! " he yelled, brandishing a revolver. " Mon, where the devil are you going ? "

" I'm going to see what's happened to one of our Batteries ! Where's the Boche ? " I answered.

" Aboot two hundred yairds doon the road ! "

I told Thompson to turn the car round, stop the engine, and wait for me. Grasping my torch and revolver and pleasantly warmed by the whisky, I walked boldly on. Toc 3's side road was only fifty yards further on. I pictured them feverishly pulling out under the very noses of the Boche ; there seemed every likelihood of a scrap once the Boche heard the engines of their Four-Wheel-Drives* start up. Never mind, it was all in the day's work. I turned into the road in which the position lay; it was strafed to blazes—the F.W.Ds. would never be able to pull the guns away over such a surface. Toc 3 would have to blow up their guns and come away without them.

I soon reached the position. To my amazement the sunken road was absolutely deserted. The gun-pits were empty ; the birds had flown ! I flashed my torch into the Fighting Post. Empty ! save for splashes of blood on the floor and a litter of field dressings.

* A powerful type of lorry used for hauling six-inch hows.

As I hurried back to the car I wondered bitterly why Toc 3 hadn't let us know they had managed to get away.

"Seen anything o' the Boche?" whispered the officer. "We've just got orders to dig in hereaboots."

"Why don't you go to the sunken road where our Battery was? There's plenty of wire just in front of the gun-pits and half-a-dozen good dug-outs."

"Right! Thanks, good-bye!"

"Good-bye! Good luck!" I echoed.

Thompson gave the starting handle a turn; the noise of the engine rang out through the cold stillness with startling distinctness. A sudden burst of machine-gun fire which sounded barely a hundred yards away startled me out of my wits. It was so totally unexpected; hitherto everything had been so quiet. The bullets seemed to swish all around us. Thompson let in the clutch with a jerk; the Vauxhall leapt away and for the next five hundred yards he drove like one possessed.

Before the war Thompson had driven a landaulette belonging to an old lady who lived near Manchester and the Colonel was always grumbling at him because he drove so slowly. I wondered what the old lady would have said had she been with us then.

I got back to find that an unexpected diversion had occurred. A runner had just arrived from Toc 2 with a note from Aglionby to say his men were very tired and that he could get no horses with which to pull his guns out, so could he stay where he was for the night and pull out in the morning?

The Colonel was writing a furious reply to tell him to do his utmost to pull out at once; we sent off one of our own D.Rs. with a copy to make doubly sure he got it.

.   .   .   .

Poor Aglionby! It was not until afterwards that we learnt how magnificently he had fought his Battery throughout the day ; a brief account of his doings will not be out of place :—

" About 1.30 p.m. masses of Germans were seen from the battery position moving about on the ridge west of Lagnicourt, some going N.W. towards Noreuil, others S.W. towards Morchies. These masses were engaged by Captain Aglionby who observed from the top of the Mess dug-out about 100 yards from the guns, range 2500 yards. Many direct hits were seen, and heavy casualties inflicted, especially on the men moving S.W., who eventually turned back.

" About 2.15 p.m. 2nd Lieut. Callis, who was manning a reserve O.P. about half-a-mile from the Battery, reported large masses of enemy north of Lagnicourt ; these were engaged and heavy casualties inflicted.

" About 2.45 p.m. 2nd Lieut. Callis observed Germans advancing in waves down the Lagnicourt valley towards the Noreuil-Morchies road. He was forced by machine-gun fire and by the fact that there were no infantry between him and the enemy to evacuate the O.P. Noticing on his way back that the Brown Line was also void of infantry, he collected a few stragglers and posted them in shell-holes on the flanks of the Battery position. Meanwhile, Capt. Aglionby engaged the oncoming masses and finally had the satisfaction of seeing the whole lot scatter and run back over the sky line towards Lagnicourt. During this time the enemy brought heavy machine-gun fire to bear on the position.

" About 4 p.m. a heavy attack developed from the same direction. The enemy massed in great quantities and, on being engaged by the Battery, split up into small parties and advanced towards the Brown Line with great determination. An enemy field gun was brought up and fired at the Battery over open sights ; several of its shells went through the camouflage of one gun-pit and several fell close to Capt. Aglionby who turned two howitzers on to it and silenced it with two salvoes. It was difficult to stop the advance of some of the small parties of the enemy who reached the Brown Line. Others entered Maricourt Wood about 400 yards from the Battery position. There appeared to be no infantry between the Battery and the enemy but the subaltern officers of the Battery not required for work on the guns collected stragglers and gunners and distributed them in shell holes behind the wire encircling the Battery position. A desultory fire was opened at such Germans as could be seen and Capt. Aglionby contented himself with putting down a heavy barrage on the Noreuil-Morchies road, which effectually prevented further supports from coming up. The parties in the Brown Line and Maricourt Wood apparently gave up all attempts at further advance, for no further attack was made.

" At 6.30 p.m. large masses were again seen assembling N.W. of Lagnicourt ; they were engaged and dispersed.

" In all during the day 800 rounds were fired at ranges varying from 1200 to 2500 yards."*

Aglionby was recommended for an " immediate " D.S.O. (which, shameful to say, he did not get). Callis won a bar to his M.C., and Graham, who did admirable work in the Battery, won an M.C.

Hugh Aglionby, who earned a magnificent reputation

* From the account the Colonel submitted when he recommended Aglionby for a D.S.O.

that day, was one of those lucky individuals who takes life exactly as it comes. It was told of him that a year or two before the war he booked a passage for a holiday trip to America and went down to the docks to join his boat. Arrived at the docks, however, he conceived a sudden dislike for the appearance of the boat that was going to America but saw a very nice looking one at the other end of the dock. He climbed aboard with his suit-case in his hand—and went to China instead!

Unlike the majority of the Brigade, he could face the Colonel without turning a hair. When we were resting at Gézaincourt the Colonel, really angry, sent for him and strafed him up hill and down dale on account of the filthy appearance of his Battery car. Aglionby stood silent until the Colonel had finished whereupon he remarked in a slightly bored tone, but with perfect sincerity, " It may be dirty, sir, but I guarantee it can race yours to Amiens ! "

. . . .

The Sergeant-Major came in and reported that our two lorries were loaded up so we sent them off under Benwell's (the Orderly Officer) charge to the Bapaume Brickworks, which had been allotted to us as reserve headquarters.

Outside in the roadway there was considerable confusion. A Heavy Battery and the remains of a Field Battery had turned up ; both claimed the pits beside our headquarters as their reserve position. After five minutes' argument, during which the beautiful horses impatiently pawed the ground as though the stupidity of human beings was beyond them, the Heavies gave way to the Field and departed for a position farther to the rear.

The Field gunners unlimbered their guns and set to work to lay out the line of fire ; ten minutes later they were firing madly away though heaven only knows what they were firing at.

The O.C. of the Battery—a subaltern—seemed so dazed that we took him into the mess and gave him a good meal. He was the only officer survivor of his Battery, which had been in action in front of Toc 3 near Louverval. The Boche had over-run them early in the day, but not before the gunners had repulsed them twice with Lewis guns and rifles. How they had managed to get any guns away he didn't know—only three had been fit to move, the other three were lying smashed to pieces on the position. After he had had something to eat he bucked up considerably and went out on to the road bank twice to see if the Boches were in sight !

An officer of Toc 2 arrived to say that they had got all the hows. away except one which was hopelessly ditched in a shell hole. They had borrowed horses to try to shift it but in vain ; only a tank could pull it out so they had removed the dial sight and breech block and left it.

Finally, one of the D.Rs. who had been posted as a look-out on the Bapaume road came and reported that Toc 1's pieces had gone safely by.

It was long past midnight and there was now nothing for us to wait for ; all our Batteries were well on their way to their new positions so the car was summoned and the Colonel and I drove away from the spot that had been our happy home for over six months. It was a sad moment and, as I looked back and saw the vivid flashes of the Field guns firing away in the midst of our once spotless headquarters, it seemed—as indeed it nearly was—the beginning of the end of all things. . . .

MARCH 22ND, 1918

All that was left of the Brickfields was a series of stout brick vaults which had been allotted to another Brigade in addition to ourselves. Having got there first, the other Brigade had occupied the best vaults and left us with the ones facing the Boche. We were far too weary to worry about such a trifle; my batman had nobly rigged up my bed but the Doc was sleeping in it, so I turned in on the floor. Considering that the Brickfields had been occupied during the past year by the A.S.C., the standard of comfort was very low; the vaults were atrociously damp and slightly niffy.

I slept intermittently till 5 a.m. by which time I was so fed up with people stumbling over me that I got up.

The battle re-opened at daybreak.* Gardiner had been performing prodigies of valour during the night and we were " through " to all our six-inch how. Batteries who were all in action once more in the fields north of Fremicourt. The Olympians had wisely decided that a moving battle was no fit place for such sluggish creatures as nine-twos: consequently Toc 1's and Toc 6's pieces were now crawling across the Somme en route for the very back of the front; their officers and gunners were detailed off to reinforce Toc 2, Toc 3

Extract from Third Army Intelligence Summary of 21-3-18.
" The enemy apparently attacked this morning with eight fresh divisions on the front between the Canal du Nord and Fontaine. . . . It is to be anticipated that ten divisions, possibly including the four originally holding the front, will continue the attack to-morrow."

Toc 5 Retreating along the Bapaume-Albert Road
(Note the "Cat" and the Camouflage).

Reproduced by permission of the Imperial War Museum.

and Toc 4. Toc 5, whose six-inch guns were far less mobile than six-inch hows., were still pulling in south of Fremicourt. Like the nine-twos, however, they too were withdrawn a day or two later.

I do not remember much of the incidents of the day ; during the morning the Colonel went off round the Batteries leaving me to talk to Corps Heavies with whom we were once more, unfortunately, in perfect communication and targets came through in shoals. The Major of Toc 1, very fed up about his nine-twos, came to suggest that the other batteries of the Brigade, instead of borrowing his officers and men, could each lend him one of their hows. so that he could form a three-gun battery and carry on the good work. The Colonel agreed to this most practical suggestion and Toc 2, Toc 3 and Toc 4 were each ordered to hand over forthwith one how. complete with stores. The Major also wanted to take a party back in a lorry to try to salve his firing beams—massive steel girders on which nine-twos are erected—which they had been forced to leave behind owing to lack of lorries but as it was a six-hour job to dig them out and as the Boche was already in Morchies, the Colonel wouldn't hear of it.

As a good example of what an Adjutant is expected to know and to do, the following note arrived from one of our Batteries ; the runner who brought it said he had been told to wait for an answer :—

"We have taken up two pits at the approximate position you gave us but they are not numbered 267 so our map board is no use. We have received 200 rounds of ammunition minus the tubes. What is to be my Centre Line ? A map is required. Where are we to run telephone wires to ? I have no wire at all. I have no rations on hand for to-day."

Throughout the day the Boche advanced slowly but surely. Vaulx fell and in the afternoon we heard that the infantry were fighting around our old headquarters in Beugny. Luckily we were still in blissful ignorance that on our immediate right the Fifth Army was in full retreat.

During the afternoon Toc 3 and Toc 4 performed a feat which earned them a mention in the *Times*.*
Major Clark, observing from a crest a few hundred yards in front of his Battery, engaged the Boche pouring out of Vaulx at a range of about a thousand yards. I met him soon afterwards riding back on his Douglas to look for a new position. White with excitement and lack of sleep, he told me he saw his shells cutting great lanes in the Boche ranks as a scythe mows down the grass.

One scene is fixed indelibly in my mind's eye. I was standing on a high bank which commanded a fine view up the Cambrai road as far as Fremicourt. The light was just beginning to fail. Batteries were in action all around; even the distant fields sparkled with countless tiny flashes. A heavy barrage was bursting on the far ridge. Along the road a slow stream of traffic was moving towards Bapaume and beyond, first waves of the tide that rolled westwards for days and days. Here

**From " The Times " of 29th March, 1918.*

" No troops could possibly have behaved better than the gunners, and in this I would especially say that I do not mean field gunners alone. The Royal Garrison Artillery has borne itself magnificently. The strain upon the men with the heavy guns has been stupendous, and their endurance, their resource, and their courage have been beyond all praise. . . . Two batteries of six-inch howitzers, near Morchies, completely broke up a heavy German attack. One battery, firing from the open at 1000 yards range, and the other from cover at 1700, got on to masses of Germans trying to advance and completely broke them up, and the attack utterly failed. . . ."

and there a battery in retreat, walking wounded in twos and threes, an odd lorry or two, a staff car carrying with undignified speed the dignified sign of Corps Headquarters, a column of horse transport and a biggish batch of German prisoners captured by the 51st Division. The procession reminded me of a cinematograph film; it was with something approaching a shock that I realised everything was moving the wrong way.

Rumour was busy; it was said that the Boche cavalry was actually in sight, first on the far ridge towards Vaulx, next coming over the crest of the Cambrai road. People turned their heads and stared curiously into the distance but there was no panic.

I stood watching the unforgettable scene for ten minutes; it was too sad for words.

I was joined by Shore, a subaltern of Toc 1, who a fortnight earlier had been put in charge of Corps Heavies' reserve ammunition dump, hard by. When I had last seen him he couldn't say too much about his job; there was nothing to do; he was messing with the A.S.C.; never in his life had he had such quantities of strawberry jam and kidneys. But the times had changed and he must have been watching the retreat with mixed feelings for Corps Heavies had just ordered him and his men to hold on " for the present " and five minutes later his telephone line back to them had gone " dis "! I left him practising rapid-loading with his revolver; half-an-hour later his dump was put up by a stray shell and he had the unpleasant job of trying to put it out.

In the late afternoon we got orders to move our Batteries into positions in map-square H 26, *i.e.* half-a-mile west of Bapaume.

Corps Heavies were still in their old quarters at Grévillers ; the Colonel decided that we should go there too as Corps Headquarters were moving out and there were sure to be plenty of superior billets to let.

We loaded up our lorries once more and " beat it " through Bapaume which was being strafed by a very big high-velocity gun. Needless to say the Albert Road corner, usually so crowded with infantry officers patiently awaiting a lift to Amiens, was deserted save for a solitary " Red-cap " clad in a tin-hat and directing the traffic.

29 C.C.S., just outside Grévillers, was being evacuated. A fleet of 'buses stood outside—incidentally stopping all traffic—and nurses and wounded were clambering up on top. To Albert I heard they were going.

When we reached Grévillers we found that all the best billets had been snaffled by the infantry so we took possession of a miserable hovel beside the ruins of the church ; Corps Heavies were living in a suite of luxurious Nissen huts on top of the hill, barely a hundred yards away.

The Colonel and the Orderly Officer went off in the car to reconnoitre battery positions ; I went up the hill to Corps Heavies to see the Staff Captain about rations and ammunition supply.

As I climbed up the broad duckboard path, neatly covered with strips of rabbit wire to prevent you from slipping, I felt even more like a tramp than usual. The lawn was as neat as ever ; the garden, fringed with its decorous row of huts, had never looked better. In the middle of the lawn stood the trophy, a Boche pip-squeak, resplendent in its new coat of paint. Above it on a line dangled a row of magpies shot by the

Reconnaisance Officer with the Brigade Major's gun. Sleek gentlemanly clerks, carrying papers and what not, hurried in and out of the offices. Even the huts, with their tarred and sanded roofs, daintily camouflaged ends, and neat notice boards, eyed me askance. I entered a hut labelled AMMUNITION OFFICER where friend Smithers told me—um yes—that six-inch ammunition was very scarce owing to the large amounts that had been dumped on the reserve positions, and—er— handed over to the Boche. However there were a few thousand rounds lying at Puisieux; we could draw from these if we liked —um yes—but they weren't likely to be in very good condition as they had been salved from the Somme. Failing that we would have to send our lorries 15 miles back to the railhead at Acheux where ammunition was being sent up as fast as possible; it wasn't considered safe to bring the trains any closer to the line—um yes—under the present circumstances.

Rations were to be drawn from the railhead at Achiet-le-Grand which was being evacuated. Everyone could take as much as was wanted; no indents were required.

Next I went into the Counter-Battery Office where one could always rely on hearing the very latest news.

" Anyone in ? " I asked a clerk, who was quietly packing up a typewriter. " Oh no, sir," in a surprised tone, " they are all in the Mess having dinner."

I went into their pretty Mess.

" Good evening, sir ! " said I to the Counter-Battery Colonel.

" Hullo, Ninety ! Sit down and have dinner with us !" said the Counter-Battery Orderly Officer affably.

" I haven't got time ! "

"Have a drink, then! By the way, excuse the candles—the electric light plant's being packed up, you know. Beastly nuisance shifting, isn't it?"

So I sat down and passed a pleasant ten minutes hearing how Major R—— and his Battery had been captured intact (an unfounded libel, but very amusing if you knew Major R——); how the Americans were arriving in thousands; how we had attacked up north on a huge scale and captured Lens and Ostend; how none of the big mines in the Cambrai road had been blown as the keys were kept in Demicourt and, by the time the sappers sent over for them, Demicourt had been surrounded and captured. And, more truthfully, how — Brigade had lost more than half its guns; how poor A. and young B. and old C. and many more besides had been killed.

We discussed the unaccountable silence of the Boche artillery on the night of the 21st and why, even granted that they were busily engaged moving forward their guns, they did not make use of their long range railway pieces. Two or three nine-four-five H.Vics dropping shells on the Bapaume-Cambrai road would have made all the difference—as it was, everything had been able to get away undisturbed. And what a difference it would have made, too, had we had a couple of six-inch guns snugly dug in at the Bapaume end of the Cambrai road firing away straight down it, for it ran straight as a die for miles and miles.

After a final whisky and soda I crept back to our hovel, wrote a few letters to the Batteries and so to bed.

MARCH 23RD.

" Wake up ! Wake up ! "

I stirred drowsily.

The Colonel shook me. " Wake up ! " he said abruptly.

Still half asleep, I sat up rubbing my eyes. It was quite dark ; the atmosphere of the room was thick : the Doc and the Signal Officer were snoring softly on the floor beside me. Outside, but far away, I could hear the galloping noise of heavy gunfire.

" What's up, sir ? " I asked, closing my eyes again and nodding.

" Read this ! " The Colonel thrust a message form into my hand and switched on his electric lamp.

Something in his tone aroused me. I looked at the paper and read with a shock of dismay :—

"The enemy has broken through at Mory. We have no troops left to put in the line. Sixth Corps."

That was all ; I remember the utter despair I felt. We had done our best. . . . Was this the end ? . . .

The Colonel was lacing his boots. " Wake up the others and tell them to dress," he said bitterly. " Tell an officer of each Battery to stand by the 'phone. I'm going up to Corps Heavies to see what they are going to do."

" Did the message come through them, sir ? "

" Yes ! " The Colonel took up his lamp and went out.

Good lord, it couldn't be true ! And yet, with that infernal gunfire in the middle of the night, anything might be happening. . . . Oh, damn the Sixth Corps !

I woke the others and told them the news ; we dressed silently and I think we half expected the Boche to be upon us that very minute.

I stood by the doorway watching and listening ; away to the north-east the sky was flickering incessantly. How the guns were pounding away! Around Grévillers everything was still. Suddenly a great flash lit up the night. Bang! Bang! Bang! Bang!—a sixty-pounder Battery at the end of the village had opened fire. The shells tore through the cold night air with a hollow blasting roar ; the ruins echoed and re-echoed ; a flock of startled birds rose from the church and wheeled and wheeled over my head. A six-inch how. battery just in front opened up. What were they shooting at ? What was happening ?

Then I saw the light of the Colonel's lamp coming back down the duckboard path.

" It's only an S.O.S. ! " he cried scornfully. " Corps Heavies are trying to find out who sent that message— someone ought to be shot. We've just spoken to Sixth Corps. The Guards Division is in the line at Mory ; it's only an S.O.S. Are those officers on the 'phone ? "

The Colonel took up the receiver. " Yes—who's that ? Officer, Toc 4 ? S.O.S. on the Corps on our left ; take down this target. Mory, M-o-r-y. Damn it, M-O-R-Y ! Yes, Sheet 57 c, Beer twenty-one. Yes, anywhere in Mory. Get them off quick as you can. Come on exchange, give me Toc 3 now ! "

. . . . . .

After breakfast the Colonel and Gardiner went off in the car round the Batteries. I spent the morning vainly trying to discover how much ammunition they had on hand.

TOC 4 PULLING OUT ON MARCH 23RD AFTER HAVING FIRED 2000 ROUNDS INTO MORY.
Reproduced by permission of the Imperial War Museum.

MARCH 23RD, 1918

Hullo, what was that ? Bagpipes ? Drums ? Surely not ! . .

I heard the trumpets of the French Cavalry screaming their wonderful song of triumph after the Armistice but never music that so stirred the soul as that of the sobbing, skirling pipes of the 51st Division playing their survivors back to the Battle.

It was madly exhilarating standing there watching those grim Highlanders swing past ; every man in step, every man bronzed, resolute, unafraid. Could these be the weary, dirty, men who were limping past us yesterday in ragged twos and threes, asking pitifully how much further to Achiet-le-Grand ? It thrilled me to the depths ; I shivered with pride, it was too magnificent for words.

Who could behold such a spectacle and say that the pomp and circumstance of War is no more ?

.   .   .   .   .   .

A note came over from the Major of Toc 1 who was going strong with his borrowed six-inch hows. :—

"Am still firing on Mory, keeping well clear of the line you ordered although I think we are now behind it. Have only about 25 more rounds per how., also no lorries. Can fill up with F.W.Ds. if necessary, and I have sent to see if there is any six-inch how. ammunition in Achiet-le-Grand. I have now my 3 F.W.Ds., but should like a few lorries if possible."

Lorries, lorries, lorries ! The cry was always for more lorries, but we could do nothing for him. Corps Heavies had detailed all that they could lay hands on to go off and fetch ammunition from the railheads.

During the morning Corps Heavies moved out of their headquarters, we gratefully moved in. One could not help noticing that despite the shortage of lorries Corps Heavies were doing themselves pretty proud. Lorry after lorry rolled up to be loaded with such delightful etcetera as the electric lighting set, armchairs, and a fine kitchen range that had certainly not been paid for by its present owners. Even the trophy went off tied to the back of a lorry ; its gaily painted little wheels twinkled round so fast that it looked like a toy.

I opened our office in what had been the Brigade-Major's, and prepared to enjoy the unusual comfort of our surroundings.

Enter " Gilly "—but allow me to introduce you to him.

He is a fully fledged Temporary Captain of the A.S.C. (M.T.), and commands, not without success, the "Cats", Four-Wheel-Drives, and hundred lorries that belong to us (or, as Gilly would always have it, that are merely attached to you, old dear). Always well groomed and immaculately dressed, even under the very worst conditions, he bears a slight, very slight, resemblance to the Crown Prince and is one of the very best. His ear is a little torn ; this was done when he crashed in a shell-hole while motor-cycle racing round the Arras track in early '17. Like all the best people he is not on the sweetest of terms with Siege Park so, what with the Colonel on one side and the O.C. Siege Park on the other, he is between the devil and the deep sea though he will never commit himself by saying who is the devil. Recreations : Collecting light coloured breeches, car driving, partridge shooting. Clubs : Sixth Corps Officers', Behagnies (Life Member) ; Army and Navy Leave Club, Paris (Country Member).

"Hullo, B. ! " said he, " Busy ? Where's the Old Man ? "

HATCH, M.C., D.C.M., M.M.　　GRAINGER.

"GILLY"

MARCH 23RD, 1918

" Not very ! Out, thank goodness ! What about a small spot ? . . . Oh, by the way, you know the ration dump at Achiet-le-Grand is being evacuated ? Well, the Old Man wants you to send a lorry there *tout de suite* to pick up as much rum as poss. and dish it out to the batteries. It's a jolly good idea if no one else has thought of it and the Batteries will be damned glad of it during the next two or three nights if I'm not mistaken. And don't forget to leave a jar or two here, Gilly ! "

" Right-ho, old dear. It shall be done ! "

Exit Gilly.

. . . . . .

The above has a sequel; in its proper sequence it should come several pages later but it would be a pity to spoil a good story.

Late that night my 'phone rang.

" O.C. Toc 1, sir ! " the exchange told me.

" Adjutant here, sir ! " I cried sleepily.

" Hullo, is that you ? " said the Major of Toc 1 coldly. " You know those rum jars you very kindly sent us this morning ? "

" Yes, sir ; you mean the ones the Colonel told you to keep unopened until we get on the move again ? " I interposed politely.

" Yes, those are the ones," replied the Major hastily. Well, that isn't the point ! "

" No, sir ? "

" The point is that they don't contain rum at all; they contain Nut Oil for Chinese Labourers ! "

And the remarkable part of the affair was that during the next hour Toc 2, Toc 3 and Toc 4 all rang up to make the same complaint !

. . . . .

The Colonel and Gardiner came back about noon; Gardiner burst into the office, his face one big grin.

"What d'you think?" he cried. "Toc 2 are running the Bapaume Canteen!"

"What?" I exclaimed.

"Toc 2 are in action in the Canteen grounds just beside the marquees and the E.F.C. people are clearing out! They wanted to set it on fire but old Aglionby wouldn't let them. Toc 2's Quartermaster-Sergeant is in charge and he's giving everything away! Have a cigarette!"

He tossed me an unopened tin of De Reszkes.

"I'd advise you to go down before it's too late," he added. "Ask the Colonel for the car; we've brought back with us a case of bubbly, two cases of whisky and umpteen boxes of Coronas!"

The Colonel came in.

"May I have the car to go to Toc 2, sir?" I faltered.

"Yes," he growled.

The news had spread like wildfire; as Thompson and I were starting the Sergeant-Major came running out of his billet.

"May I come with you, sir?"

"Jump in, Sergeant-Major!"

It did one's heart good to see the happy faces we met on the road. Every lorry driver had a pile of cigarette tins on the seat beside him. Every infantry soldier had his pockets bulging with them. Even the walking wounded had their arms full. Everyone was laughing.

The scene outside the great Canteen was wonderful; it might have been Christmas eve. A queue of lorries and G.S. wagons and cars and S.A.A. carts and every other sort of cart stretched for hundreds of yards down

TOC 2 IN ACTION BESIDE THE CANTEEN. STANDING BY TO FIRE INTO BAPAUME, MARCH 23RD.
Reproduced by permission of the Imperial War Museum.

the road. In almost every case they were unattended ; their drivers were inside seeking something for nothing.

On the grass in front of the Canteen were Toc 2's howitzers, drawn up in line twenty yards apart and firing steadily away, one round per battery per minute.

Across the road I saw a party of them with their tin-hats at rakish angles, posing for the Official Photographer of all people.* Heavens, look at that Number Two pulling the lanyard with a long Pantello in his mouth and a bottle of Bass in his other hand !

The officers of Toc 2 were dining in an outhouse and had reached the sweets course ; before each one of them was set a big open tin of peaches. A confused medley of shouts greeted me.

" Hullo ! Here's the Adj. ! What does he want ? Come in ! Go away ! Sit down ! Have some fruit ! "

" What can we offer you ? " asked Aglionby gravely. " Lime juice, whisky, gin, beer, stout, champagne, wincarnis, port, benedictine, or crême de menthe ? "

" Come and have a look ! " said Aglionby to me a few minutes later, " It's as much as we can do to keep our soldiers on the guns."

We walked into the marquee. The mob inside was growing unruly ; the Quartermaster-Sergeant of Toc 2 and his assistants were unable to cope with the rush. Men were clambering over the counters ; others, already across, were pulling down piles of boxes to see what was on top.

" It's getting a bit too popular," remarked Aglionby gloomily. " Help yourself while there's time ! "

* Sir Philip Gibbs, I believe. At any rate, whoever he was, he was put under arrest by Toc|4 for being in possession of a camera

An E.F.C. attendant came up to Aglionby.

"I'm going now, sir," said he cheerfully. "No objection—everyone 'elping themselves as 'ts better our lads 'ave it instead of them 'Uns but pleash purra guard over—hic—whisky or theshe chaps won't be 'alf blind!"

On the way back we examined our spoils. The Sergeant-Major had a case of tins of Café-au-lait, 17 tins of biscuits and five pounds of tobacco. I had 1160 cigarettes, six dozen Gillette blades, one Ingersoll watch, one patent combined tin-opener and corkscrew, one whole roast chicken, two bottles of Grand Marnier and one package which, on investigation, was found to contain 144 boxes of Beecham's Pills. At a guinea a box these would have been worth £151 4s.

A noisy luncheon party was in progress in our hovel. The menu : Prawns in aspic.
>Cold boiled ham.
>Pineapple and tinned cream.

>Pol Roger '06.
>Johnny Walker.

". . . Yes, I'm a pretty good hand at choosing battery positions!" I heard the Colonel saying with a chuckle.

．　　．　　．　　．　　．　　．

The afternoon passed uneventfully; when the Colonel saw how much room there was and how all the men's huts were fitted up with beautiful wire beds he told me to tell the Batteries that, if they liked, they could each send a party of fifty men back to us for a good night's rest.

Night fell; it was cold and starry; when the moon rose it would be a perfect night for bombing.

MARCH 23RD, 1918

The Sergeant-Major came into the office.

"These parties from the Batteries have arrived, sir! I've handed over six Nissen huts to them but some of the men prefer to sleep underground in the big dug-out. And there's a big party of reinforcements for the Brigade just turned up, sir; there's no nominal roll with them. Will you keep them here to-night and post them to Batteries in the morning?"

"Yes, Sergeant-Major, you might make out a nominal roll and—"

CRASH!

God, what was that? We both ducked blindly. Huge splinters burst through the hut, travelling with incredible speed. Outside the branches were snapping off the trees as though torn down by a hurricane.

For fifteen seconds an awful silence reigned throughout the camp broken only by the falling of branches and stones. Then a pitiful chorus of moaning and shouting slowly broke out; the Sergeant-Major ran to the door.

"It hit the hut where I put the reinforcements!" he cried.

. . . . . .

One can hear a howitzer fire and one generally has time to dart for cover or otherwise prepare oneself; one can also hear the sharp distinctive bark of a high velocity gun several seconds before the arrival of its shell but this gun had given us no warning at all; its shell had landed in our midst literally with the suddenness of a flash of lightning. What was it, we asked in frightened whispers.* How soon would it fire again?

---

* Counter-Battery afterwards told us it was a 9.45 inch gun on a railway mounting firing from the railway somewhere near Havrincourt at a range of about ten miles.

The casualties inflicted by that one shell were fearful ; apart from some fifteen killed and wounded an indefinite number were so completely blown to pieces that they were unidentifiable.*

Something had to be done for the wounded ; it was impossible to telephone for ambulances as all the lines had gone so I volunteered to go off to 29 C.C.S. and fetch one ; anything was better than sitting still in a Nissen hut waiting for the next shell to arrive. Fulton, the Artillery Clerk, said he would come with me.

The Doc and Benwell and the Sergeant-Major and several more set to work to dress the wounded ; Gardiner and his linesmen went out to get the lines through and the Colonel was walking about fearlessly as though nothing had happened ; Fulton and I put on our tin hats and hurried off.

It was not a pleasant walk. A second shell fell short just as we were starting and seemed to have landed exactly where we were going.

It had ; on the road a bare hundred yards from the church gaped a monstrous hole 6 yards across and deep

* Thereby hangs a sad tale. Many weeks later we received a letter from a woman in England asking if we could give her any news about her son from whom she had not heard since he sailed to France. She had written to the R.G.A. Depot at the Base who had referred her to us, stating that according to their records her son had departed for our Brigade on March 20th, together with a draft of forty other men.

How could one adequately reply that her son was one of the poor fellows blown to pieces ?

As an example of how closely the tragic is allied to the grotesque, Bombadier White, the Brigade Medical Orderly, told me that the most horrible sight of all was that of an unwounded but frightened reinforcement whose bully beef tin, driven inwards by a shell splinter, had burst and scattered its repulsive-looking contents over his stomach !

in proportion. Half in it lay a headless despatch rider; the petrol from the twisted tank of his motor-cycle was sizzling on the hot cylinder.

We hurried on; a third shell tore over our heads with a rush like that of an express train and burst on the hillside, but well short of our camp. " That's just about where our linesmen have got to! " remarked Fulton. The splinters seemed to travel for hundreds of yards; we both fancied we had seen the flash of the gun in the eastern sky.

29 C.C.S. was still being evacuated; there were plenty of ambulances but it was impossible to get hold of one. An R.A.M.C. Staff-Sergeant who was marshalling them told me I couldn't have one without permission from his Commanding Officer so I wandered through the crowded wards in search of him. They reeked of blood and chloroform and iodine; the cries and groans of the wounded mingled with the too frequent crashes of the five-nines that were bursting close outside. Several field batteries were now in action just behind; as they fired the hospital huts shivered and shook incessantly. At last I got my chit; the R.A.M.C. Staff-Sergeant gave me an ambulance, shouted to the driver to be back as quick as he could, and off we went.

The driver drove mechanically; his face was white with dust, his eyes were bloodshot and half closed. We swerved round the big shell hole; the driver saw the despatch rider and threw out his clutch as though about to pull up. " Dead! " I shouted; he nodded and drove on.

Close beside the church the Sergeant-Major and a small party were waiting with the stretchers which were handed in quickly and carefully.

"Right away, driver! Come back for another load!" he shouted.

The Sergeant-Major was always splendid at times like these; I remember thinking how well he deserved the Médaille Militaire for which he had just "clicked".

The 9.45 had not fired again; we were hoping that its gunners were packing up in preparation for a forward move but our hopes were vain for soon after midnight she fired six more rounds into the village and three more soon after daybreak.

Boche 'planes were humming overhead all night long and great bombs were dropping north, south, east and west; it was a terrible night and we all thought it heralded a tremendous new Boche attack in the morning.

MARCH 24TH, 1918

But, strange to say, next day there was a distinct pause; on our front at least the Boche seemed to have temporarily over-reached himself.

The Battery "resting parties" returned thankfully to their Batteries.

During the morning we heard that things were going very badly down south and that another big retreat, right back across the Somme and the Ancre, was likely. I think people were almost relieved to hear this; the country where we were was so utterly waste that anything seemed better than settling down there for the inevitable months of trench warfare that would follow.

We prepared for whatever might turn up by sorting all the stores we had brought with us and dumping all the rubbish. The Colonel ever after swore that the Sergeant-Major had loaded up the rubbish and dumped the rest; it certainly was a remarkable fact that for months afterwards whenever we asked the Sergeant-Major for anything at all out of the ordinary he would invariably reply, " That was left at Grévillers—Colonel's orders, sir ! "

I did my bit by leaving behind for the Boche a pair of old gum boots in which I set half-a-dozen drawing pins, pins upwards; afterwards my conscience pricked me for fear that some of our infantry had tried them on first.

After lunch we set to work to burn all the maps and papers we could find ; it was wonderful how much Corps Heavies had managed to accumulate. Suddenly someone shouted, " Look ! X. Don's on fire ! "*

We rushed out ; it was quite true.

From our hill-top we got a wonderful view ; through our glasses we could see intrepid men running about amongst the smoke but whether they were trying to run away or put it out or set it alight (so as to prevent the Boche from getting it) we never learnt. If the latter they were certainly successful for within five minutes X. Don was a fearsome sight. An enormous column of grey smoke had ascended nearly half-a-mile into the sky ; at the top it was spreading out like a vast mushroom. The dump crackled continuously ; from where we were it sounded like thousands of sausages in a frying pan.

We passed a pleasant quarter-of-an-hour listening to the crackling and trying to guess what the various things were that were going up ; rifle ammunition or Flying Pigs or Duchesses or Mills' Bombs or Stokes' or Shrapnel or H.E. The fuzes went up like golden rain and we had a real first-class thrill when a dump of Very Lights exploded and speckled the cloudy sky with thousands of beautiful coloured lights.

Hundreds and hundreds of birds were passing by, in full flight from this strange new horror !

Nero would undoubtedly have claimed us as his own as we stood there on the trim lawn beside the idly dangling magpies, smoking expensive looted cigarettes

---

* " X. Don " was the familiar code name of the huge ammunition dump that stretched for half-a-mile along the Bapaume-Arras road.

MARCH 24TH, 1918

and gleefully watching the fireworks—though after a short time its very immensity appalled us.

The orders for us to continue the retreat arrived while X. Don was still burning ; we were to report to Corps Heavies outside Achiet-le-Grand on the Achiet-le-Petit road. This time the retreat resembled more of a rout than had previously been the case ; the roads were fairly full and everyone seemed anxious to get away as quickly as possible, regardless of anyone else—though it would be wrong to say there was a panic. Cars and lorries found themselves hung up behind such impassable things as pigeon caravans while slow-moving columns of infantry transport meandered on and off the roads where and when they pleased. A few Military Policemen dashed up and down on horseback trying to enforce some sort of order but no one took much notice and, had the Boche been able to break through with cavalry or armoured cars, the war would have ended for most of us.

The rifle fire sounded very close and everyone was wondering how many infantry there were between us and the Boche. After about half-an-hour's struggling our two lorries managed to reach the corner leading into the main Bapaume—Achiet-le-Grand road.

We came to a standstill. I jumped down to find out the reason. A cyclist on point duty at the corner said to me, " It's no good going on to Achiet along this road, sir : the bridge is down. You'll have to turn back and go round through Grévillers ! "

This was a pretty kettle of fish ; I knew it would be absolutely impossible to attempt even to turn round, let alone work our way back against the traffic on the narrow road to Grévillers (which by this time might have been captured by the Boche) so, having a faint idea of the geography of Achiet-le-Grand, I told the cyclist that the bridge was on the far side of the village and that we wanted to turn off long before we got to it.

Reluctantly he allowed us to pass and, thanks to his efforts, the road in front of us was absolutely empty. We bowled along merrily at a good ten miles an hour ; I looked back and saw that every one was following us ; come what may, we had the great advantage of being in front !

But as things turned out I was right and the cyclist was wrong ; it was easy to get through Achiet-le-Grand without going anywhere near the bridge because there wasn't one.

I parked the lorries in a side road in the middle of Achiet-le-Grand and walked off to the rendezvous to meet the Colonel who had gone on ahead in the car.

The rendezvous turned out to be a Divisional Headquarters which struck me as being a funny place for Corps Heavies to tell us to report to.

But a greater surprise was in store. The Colonel met me outside.

" Corps Heavies have washed their hands of us," he said. " It has been decided to attach us to the 40th Division until things settle down again ! "

The question of whether the Heavy Artillery should come under the orders of the Divisions like the Divisional Field Artillery was always a vexed one, and there were certainly many points in favour of it, but, at a crisis like this, it seemed absolute folly. Efficient though a Division may be, it is only asking for trouble to cast at its head at a moment's notice a Heavy Artillery Brigade which requires thousands of gallons of petrol for its lorries and tons of ammunition for its hows. as different

MARCH 24TH, 1918

from that used by the Divisional Artillery as lead from feathers.

The Colonel went inside again; I waited in blank amazement wondering what on earth was going to happen next. I saw our Brigade-Major in one of the offices; he was very fed up at the turn of events. While I was talking to him an inner door suddenly opened and two Lieutenant-Generals came out. Both looked exceedingly grave as they walked through the room; the Brigade-Major whispered that a Corps Commanders' Conference had just taken place to decide what was to be done; on our immediate right there was a tremendous gap caused by the rout of the Fifth Army and there was every likelihood of the Boche completely outflanking us.

Despite the seriousness of the situation one could not help appreciating its drama; here in this very room were the men upon whom depended not only our personal safety but possibly that of the whole British Expeditionary Force.

The Corps Commanders departed swiftly in their motors; the Colonel sent me back to guide the lorries to our new destination—the 40th Division near Bucquoy.

I walked back to the lorries; on the way I passed one of the Corps Commanders who was held up in the traffic like any other mortal.

A big mail from home had just reached us; the Sergeant-Major gave me my letters and I was interested to read, " Glad to get your letter of the 14th. Everyone at home is expecting to hear that the big German offensive has opened but we are glad you say that you don't think they will get very far."

Our progress from Achiet-le-Grand to Bucquoy was a mere crawl; we passed the huts and tents of the 40th

Division but there was nowhere where we could turn off so on we had to move with the stream.

At last, about a quarter of a mile short of Bucquoy, we came to a small side road down which we turned laboriously, pursued by the cursing of the traffic behind us which we held up for several minutes. The lorries were unloaded in a field by the roadside and the Colonel and I walked back to the Division across the waste of overgrown shell holes.

Things were extremely busy in the Divisional Artillery office ; we waited nearly ten minutes before anyone took any notice of us. Then someone introduced the Colonel to the Divisional Artillery General.

" You must excuse me," said he to the Colonel, " things are very critical just now on our sector ; my Brigade-Major will attend to your wants—there he is ! "

So the Colonel walked across to the Brigade-Major, told him where our Batteries were and what sort of guns they owned and finished up with, " By the way, we *must* have five hundred gallons of petrol by noon to-morrow at the latest."

The Brigade-Major, completely taken back, gasped, seized a pencil, jotted down on a scrap of paper " 500 gallons of petrol," and, after a short pause, said, " Oh, ha ! Right ! I'll fix up a scheme ! "

The Colonel sourly added, " Also we only have enough rations to last us till breakfast to-morrow."

The Brigade-Major jotted down " Rations, 700 men," and, after another short pause, said, " Oh, ha ! Right ! I'll fix up a scheme ! "

They looked at one another ; the utter absurdity of the situation seemed to dawn upon them—they both grinned.

MARCH 24TH, 1918

The General then came across and told the Colonel to get his guns limbered up ready to move at a moment's notice and park them on any suitable side road between Achiet-le-Grand and Logeast Wood.

"But, you know," he concluded, "the situation is changing so frequently that I may have to send you fresh orders at any minute. Leave a runner here so that I can get in touch with you at once."

The Colonel and I walked silently back to our field; now that the excitement was over the outlook had never seemed blacker.

During a supper of sorts our runner returned with a situation telegram, historically interesting enough to warrant inclusion :—

"The enemy have occupied Combles, Morval and Lesboeufs necessitating a retirement of the right of the Third Army AAA As soon as it is dark to-night the 40th Division will leave outposts on its present front line and withdraw to the following approximate line AAA H 9 central, B 27 central, B 21 central, B 9 d 6.2, where they join with the 31st Division AAA The 42nd Division as soon as it can get up will take over the above line relieving the 40th Division whose outposts will then retire through the line AAA As soon as the infantry relief is complete the G.O.C. 42nd Division will take over command of the sector from the G.O.C. 40th Division when the Divisional Sector will pass from the command of the VI Corps to the IV Corps AAA 40th Div. Arty. will be relieved by 42nd Div. Arty. night 25th-26th AAA On relief 40th Div. Arty. will march direct to Douchy-les-Ayette. . . .

"7.45 p.m., March 24th. From 40th Div. Arty."

This telegram did not really affect us; it merely notified us that we were to be lightly bandied from the

40th to the 42nd Division which, by a curious coincidence, was the Division with which I spent the first year of the war and which, as fate would have it, remained with the Fourth Corps and shared its successes from that day until the Armistice, when I last saw them marching blithely to Charleroi.

The Colonel and I went off in the car to give our Batteries the news and choose a suitable side road. On the way we picked up Aglionby, the Major of Toc 1 and the Major of Toc 4. It was the maddest drive I have ever had—it was a fine moonlight night and the roads along which we drove were empty. We must have driven nearly into Bapaume. We could see the flashes of batteries on all sides of us but whether they were British or Boche we neither knew nor cared. Nothing seemed to matter; such was the reaction after the stress and strain of the last three days. Once we came to a dead end so we turned round and drove back the way we had come; in the middle of the road yawned a large shell hole which certainly had not been there when we had passed five minutes earlier. The Vauxhall took it in its stride. Once a field battery suddenly opened fire from behind the hedge alongside the road and almost blew us out of the car. I fell asleep and woke up to find that the road for the hows. to be parked had already been chosen and that we were on our way back to our headquarters.

The congestion, which had been bad enough in the afternoon, was now so much worse that the traffic was absolutely immovable. The Colonel jumped out of the car and walked on ahead, cursing right and left. The chief cause of the trouble was a Heavy Battery which had tried to " bank " round a Field Battery—the result was that things were at a complete deadlock and the drivers, instead of trying to straighten it up, were asleep in their saddles ! They soon woke up, however, when the Colonel addressed them and after much shouting and swearing they made a narrow lane through which Thompson was just able to drive. For the next mile the traffic was stationary but the car was so narrow that we were able to creep along in low gear. Nearly everyone was asleep ; no one seemed to care in the least how long they stayed there. The Colonel became furiouser and furiouser and vented the full force of his wrath on a cringing lorry driver who had fallen asleep at his wheel, thereby leaving a gap of several hundred yards between his lorry and the next one in front.

We reached our field and turned in thankfully in an old tent which the excellent Sergeant-Major had "won". I was hardly asleep when a runner arrived from the Division with fresh orders. The situation had materially changed ; our Batteries were to continue the retreat at dawn and put Logeast Wood between them and the Boche.

The Colonel and Thompson and I were the only ones at Brigade who knew where our Batteries were to be found ; the orders were too urgent to entrust to either of the despatch riders—excellent though they always were—who might take hours to find everyone so I volunteered to go the round on one of their motor-cycles.

The Colonel agreed ; he seemed pretty well exhausted but, what with the new excitement and the sleep in the car, I felt perfectly fresh and fit.

I set off ; the traffic on the main road was still at a standstill and the only difference I noticed was that the gap between the two lorries had closed up. It was a difficult ride ; the Triumph was not going well and the clutch was out of action ; time and again I bumped against horses or scraped my knuckles on the side of some wagon or lorry I was trying to pass. In the middle of Achiet-le-Grand the engine suddenly gave up the ghost ; after I had wasted five precious minutes vainly trying to entice it back again I shoved the bike into the ditch and left it.

My luck was in, however. At the far end of the village I passed a shed beneath which stood half-a-dozen beautiful gleaming Triumphs. I crept up to them—joy ! no one was about—and chose the newest-looking one. I pulled it off its stand, pushed it silently into the road, turned on the petrol, " tickled " the carburetter and vigorously kicked the kick-starter. Horrors, it wouldn't start ! At that very moment a man came out of the house and walked past the shed into the road. Blind panic struck me ; I was just about to leave the bike and run away when a far better idea came into my head. The man was walking past without paying very much attention to me ; I saw on his arm a couple of stripes and the blue and white badge of the Signal Service—he must be a Despatch Rider, and possibly even the owner of the bicycle I was borrowing. Never mind, chance it !

" Corporal ! " I called sternly, " Will you help me to start my bike—she's a bit cold ? "

He came to my side, injected a squirt of petrol into the cylinder—of course, how stupid of me !—and jumped on the kick-starter. The engine immediately started up with a roar.

" Thanks awfully ! " I shouted, getting astride.

" You're welcome, sir ! " he shouted back, when he must have realised.

"HI, YOU!" he yelled, "That's MY bike!"

But he was too late. . . .

I found the officers of Toc 1 and Toc 4 sleeping out in their valises beside their hows. In valises all men look alike so many were called but few were chosen.

I rode on, passing Toc 3 on the way, and found that Toc 2, always with an eye to the main chance, had occupied a row of comfortable huts on the eastern outskirts of Logeast Wood. The officers were having a merry evening on the remains of the Bapaume Canteen so I joined them once more for a few minutes and then, utterly worn out, wended my weary way back to the tent which I reached about 3 a.m. and by one minute past I was sleeping like a log.

MARCH 25TH, 1918.

I woke up a few hours later cold, damp, stiff. The cooks had left the firewood out in the rain and there was not a drop of petrol to spare for the fire so there would be no tea for hours and hours. Had life ever been more unbearable, I wondered, listening to the rain pattering down on the tent.

The hours wore on very slowly; the Batteries had moved at dawn and were now in action in various positions on the westerly end of the road through Logeast Wood which, by the way, was a wood only in name. It was impossible to lay lines to them; we had hardly any wire left.

At eleven o'clock a situation report arrived from the Division; our front line was practically the same as that described in the situation report of the previous evening except that we had lost about a thousand yards on the northern part of the Divisional Sector. Bapaume was now well inside the Boche lines. The telegram ended with that irritating platitude:—

"Keep well clear of above line; short shooting has been constant."

An hour later, however, a note arrived by runner from Aglionby:—

"Infantry Brigadier here reports he is not holding Sapignies and Béhagnies and has asked me to fire on them."

TOC 3 NEAR LOGEAST WOOD. JUST FIRED!

Reproduced by permission of the Imperial War Museum.

So the Boche had managed to advance another mile or two.

Gilly, who had been tearing here there and everywhere on his motor-cycle in search of petrol, happened to be with us when Aglionby's note arrived.

" By Jove ! " he said thoughtfully, " I hope they've managed to get the billiard table (from the Club at Béhagnies) away safely ! "*

In the end a lorry full of petrol tins arrived from Siege Park ; the difficulty would be its distribution for the congestion was nearly as bad as on the previous day.

We were still drawing ammunition from Puisieux but a lorry can only carry fifty rounds of six-inch how. ammunition at a time and it took anything up to six hours for it to work its way from the Batteries to the dump and back again and even then it was lucky if it got through. Our hundred lorries were by now hopelessly lost, stolen, and strayed ; at last the Colonel in despair stood at the corner by the main road and tried to buttonhole every empty lorry that went past, regardless of what unit it belonged to. On such occasions he was fluent and persuasive so he met with remarkable success ; at the end of an hour he had managed to seduce one for certain and two doubtful ones who said they would turn round at the next corner and come back.

In the early afternoon orders arrived that the Brigade was to continue the retreat at once and report to Corps Heavies again at Acheux Château, a jump of some ten miles. So the experiment of attaching us to the Division had not lasted very long !

The Colonel and Gardiner went off in the car to get the orders through to the Batteries ; I was left behind

* They had !

with a motor-cycle to superintend the departure of our own two lorries after which I was to wait " as long as possible " (in case any of our batteries should miss the Colonel and come to Brigade for orders), and then ride on to Acheux and meet the Colonel.

I pushed our lorries off within a quarter-of-an-hour and sat down on the road bank feeling very small and lonely.

The traffic was now moving with a swing ; after I had waited half-an-hour big gaps began to appear and occasional Field Batteries went past at the trot. How long was " as long as possible " I began to wonder anxiously and started up the motor-cycle to make sure it would go all right when the time came.

The traffic was getting less and less ; at last I noticed that people were apprehensively looking behind them as though expecting the Boche. Five minutes later I could stick it no longer ; I got on the motor-cycle and rode into Bucquoy.

Events were exciting indeed ; Military Policemen with drawn revolvers were directing the traffic which was now moving at a gallop. Horse transport was being sent by one road, motor transport by another. A smart, clean looking battalion of infantry had just arrived ; the soldiers were filing into the houses and gardens at the eastern end of the village. Machine-gunners were testing their machine-guns and Lewis-gunners and riflemen were making loopholes in the walls. It was obvious that the Boche was not far away.

I felt I ought to hang on a minute or two longer so I waited beside the Military Policemen. Suddenly I saw the most welcome sight of all—the Brigade car ! Thompson was driving furiously ; the Colonel, wearing his tin hat, yelled as he swept past, " They've all got away ; come on ! "

I afterwards heard that Thompson had distinguished himself by taking a wrong turning thereby driving the car through a hot Boche barrage. The road was blocked so he had to turn round and drive back through the barrage !

I followed the car ; before I had gone very far I heard behind me a sudden crackle of musketry from Bucquoy— the Boche had arrived.

For the next couple of miles we all moved along at nearly twenty miles an hour but when we had passed Puisieux the pace slowed down considerably and half-a-mile further on I caught up the Brigade lorries. I saw one of the despatch riders sitting on the tail-board so I shouted to him to hop off and take over the motor-cycle. I climbed up on the front seat beside the Artillery Clerk and promptly dozed off.

I woke up several times during the journey; I remember hearing someone shout, " Halt ! Action left ! " to a Field Battery which left the road just in front of us ; I remember seeing a battalion of infantry bivouacking in the open ; I remember seeing another cleaning out an overgrown trench—disused since 1916— with their entrenching tools ; I remember passing a notice board which announced " THIS IS SERRE " and only those who have seen can visualise the dreadful utterness of the desolation.

I remember entering Mailly-Maillet which gave me great pleasure for it contained the first complete houses I had seen for weeks. Wondering women and children stood at the gates of their cottages and watched us driving past ; they did not seem to realise what had happened.

The scenery was so different and was changing so quickly that we seemed to be in another world; it was more like going on leave than fleeing from the Boche. I remember the windmill at Colincamps and the windmill at Bertrancourt; whenever I see a windmill to-day I think of dust and lorries and flight.

I remember rattling through Bertrancourt; last time we had passed through Bertrancourt we were on our way to Gézaincourt for a fortnight's rest. I remember passing the railhead on the Bertrancourt-Acheux road which, though we would never have believed it then, was destined to be our future ammunition dump. I remember passing the big chimney on the outskirts of Acheux which the Colonel—and no one else—afterwards wanted to use as a reserve O.P.

At last we pulled up beside the Y.M.C.A. in Acheux Square. The Y.M.C.A. were giving their stock away; our men rushed in for tea and biscuits. After the sack of the Bapaume Canteen, mere giving away seemed very flat. The shops around the square were frenziedly selling off at bargain prices.

A few minutes later the Brigade car arrived; we followed it into the Château grounds, scattering right and left fat ducks and angry geese. The Colonel hurried into the Château to report to the General. Half-an-hour later we were off again but only, thank goodness, to park our lorries and hows. on the Acheux-Forceville road and billet in Forceville for the night.

The Colonel stood in the middle of Forceville marshalling the traffic like a Military Policeman; as soon as the hows., Four-Wheel-Drives and lorries were all neatly parked in line along the road he sent me back to the Château to report that all our Batteries had arrived

MARCH 25TH, 1918

safely except Toc 1, which was missing. Nothing was known of them except that they had been very short of petrol.

The General and the Brigade-Major were sitting in a large and beautifully furnished *salon*. I told them the news and was turning to go when an orderly hurried in. As I was shutting the door the General shouted, " Come back ! "

" How long will it take you to get to your Colonel ? " he asked quickly.

" About four minutes, sir."

" Then get off as quickly as you can and tell him to continue the retreat AT ONCE. The Germans captured Albert half-an-hour ago. Make for Doullens ; either the Brigade-Major or I will be at the Town Hall there to give you fresh orders. Hurry up—Forceville is only six miles from Albert ! "

I ran to my motor-cycle. Heavens, Doullens was another twelve damned miles away—some retreat, this ; would it ever stop ? I tore along the Acheux-Forceville road like the wind ; people rushed out of the way and turned round to stare at me as if I were mad.

The Colonel was still standing complacently in the middle of Forceville surveying the neatly stretched out Brigade with a proud and fatherly eye. The lorry drivers were cleaning down their lorries ; the gunners were cleaning up their guns. Billets had already been found for half the Brigade, the other half had already found its way into the estaminets.

Within twelve minutes we were all on the move again and with real dismay in our hearts.

Again I fell into a doze ; the journey seemed endless. It soon grew dark ; the road was flanked by great trees which loomed up and faded away in endless succession ; the roar of our lorry became a lullaby ; the broad road seemed to go on and on for ever like a great white ribbon. Dust and petrol vapour was everywhere ; it filled ears and eyes, nose and mouth. Kilometer stone after kilometer stone went past ; it was impossible to grasp the fact that we were in flight . . . it seemed like some great game in which distance and villages and woods all meant nothing. In the days that followed I journeyed many a dozen times to and fro along the Acheux-Doullens road but never again did it seem so endless and we so small. Once we stopped ; I woke up to find that some big gun in front of us had fallen off the road ; our lorries could only just creep round.

We hurried on through Louvencourt and Vauchelles and Marieux and Sarton ; between Sarton and Orville a despatch rider overtook us.

" Nine-O Brigade ? " he shouted.

" Yes ! "

" Here's a letter from Corps Heavies ! "

The Colonel read it ; we were to park for the night in Orville where the men were to be given billets ; at 9 a.m. in the morning the Colonel was to report for orders at the Town Hall, Doullens.

We soon found billets for most of the men. The car was driven off the road into a field and the Colonel lighted his primus stove and cooked our supper—twopenny soup squares and champagne. After supper the Colonel and Gardiner prepared to spend the night in the car but Gilly, Benwell and I partially unloaded a lorry, swept it out and unrolled our valises in it. While we were at work the Colonel strolled over.

"Call yourself soldiers?" he asked, sniffing contemptuously. "I want two of you to be up at six and push off on motor-cycles to see if you can find Toc 1. One of you search the roads the way we came; the other towards Authie and Souastre. Don't get captured."

So we turned in quarrelling vigorously as to which of us should not get up at six.

.   .   .

MARCH 26TH, 1918

" Come on, come on ! " shouted the Colonel angrily. Gilly, Benwell and I woke up. Glory be !—it was seven o'clock !

" Get up at once ! " cried the Colonel, lifting up the back curtain, " Gardiner's been off nearly an hour ! "

Feeling rather ashamed of ourselves we dressed hastily and pushed off. It was a lovely spring morning ; the birds were singing gaily and the sun was just melting the mists. Everything seemed fresh and sweet and clean. My motor-cycle was going perfectly: a faint trail of pale blue smoke from my exhaust hung lazily a few inches above the road. No joy ride has ever been more delightful.

I met Gardiner in Marieux.

" No use going this way ! " he shouted, " I've been nearly as far as Colincamps ; the Boche is there. Not a sign of Toc 1 anywhere ! "

During the next half-hour Gilly and Benwell returned ; neither of them had any news of Toc 1 ; the roads, they said, were pretty well empty for at least ten miles.

We all began to fear the worst. Just as the Colonel was starting off for Doullens, Toc 3's Ford came tearing down the road—in it was the Major of Toc 1.

" Where's your Battery ? " cried the Colonel.

" Coming into Orville now along the Pas road, sir ! " (the one road we hadn't searched.)

The Major of Toc 1 looked more fed up than I had ever seen him before ; his uniform, his face, his tin hat were so covered with dust that he looked like a miller.

" I had to abandon one how., sir ! " he said stiffly.

"One of my Four-Wheel-Drives ran out of petrol and I couldn't get any more. We've been marching all night."

Bit by bit his story unfolded; how the congestion on the previous afternoon was so great that all the roads to Puisieux were blocked and he had been forced to turn north towards Fonquevillers with the intention of making for Doullens, where he expected he would be able to find out our whereabouts; how he had made his men march so as to economise petrol; how he had emptied his last tins into the Four-Wheel-Drives; how one of them had run dry at Ayette; how they had tried in vain to make another Four-Wheel-Drive pull two hows.; how they had finally abandoned it. And how, when they reached Pas, they found the village in an extraordinary panic; how — Corps Headquarters were frenziedly packing up; how barricades were being erected across the streets to stop the Boche armoured cars which were said to be tearing towards them along the Arras road at thirty miles an hour—our front line at Arras hardly shifted an inch, by the way—; how he and his weary gunners were actually ordered to line the heights of Pas with their rifles; how a precious ammunition lorry was commandeered by Staff Officers to move their personal kit.

The Colonel could contain himself no longer.

"Low swine!" he hissed and departed to tell Corps Heavies all about it.

Nothing seemed to matter now that Toc 1 had turned up and the Brigade was still intact.

The Colonel returned with more orders from Corps Heavies; the whole Brigade was to move at once to Mézerolles, a village five miles west of Doullens, to rest for a couple of days during which time it was to do its utmost to refit ready to enter the Battle again. Indents for important deficiencies were to be submitted at once for had not Ordnance been specially ordered to give us absolute priority?

So off we set on what turned out to be the last stage of the Great Retreat. The road was full of refugees. A Company of " Chinks " was on the march too—at least they were straggling almost from Orville into Doullens and provided a welcome comic relief. They behaved more like school children unexpectedly let out of school; they grinned at everyone and everything; they trickled in twos and threes into every estaminet they passed. Some were carrying great bundles of kit on their heads; others seemed to possess nothing more than the flimsy clothes they were wearing. Some were helping the refugees to wheel the barrow or handcart in which lay their precious household gods; others ran happily after our lorries hoping for a lift.

We paused for a minute in the outskirts of Doullens. I saw two Chinks enter a dainty fancy shop to be immediately ejected; they stood on the pavement outside the shop chattering like monkeys and gesticulating angrily.

There was the greatest activity around the Town Hall. Judging by the number of magnificent cars standing outside, important people were inside and I fancied I saw the Commander-in-Chief's car with its little Union Jack. There were huge French cars waiting too.

We did not know that Marshal Foch was there; it was not until recently that I read the following:—

" The *Matin* publishes an extract from a new book by M. Stedhane Lauzanne, editor of that paper, in which he traces in all its details the historical scene at Doullens, when Marshal Foch was appointed Commander-in-Chief of all the armies on March 26th, 1918. He writes :—

" M. Clemenceau on Sunday March 23rd, the fourth day of the German offensive on the Somme and the Oise, went to find M. Poincaré to tell him that owing to the situation it would perhaps be prudent to evacuate Paris. M. Poincaré objected.

" M. Clemenceau returned the same evening to Compiègne and telephoned M. Poincaré that General Pétain was of the same opinion as was M. Clemenceau himself.

" M. Poincaré the same night wrote M. Clemenceau to explain his objections and asked him to call a meeting of Ministers. This was held next day, but M. Clemenceau had already somewhat changed his opinion and announced to the Ministers that on March 26th an interview would be held at Doullens with a representative of the British Government, and proposed that the President of the Republic should accompany him.

" On March 26th M. Poincaré accordingly went to Doullens and was informed that Sir Douglas Haig was in conference with his Army Commanders and that it would be better not to disturb him. Accompanying M. Poincaré were MM. Clemenceau and Loucheur, as well as Marshal Foch who, in the course of conversation with M. Poincaré, informed him that serious orders had just been issued compromising an almost general retreat of the Army and involving very soon the evacuation of Paris.

" These orders seemed to produce extreme excitement in Marshal Foch who kept on repeating, ' The Boches ! Why, they can always be stopped ! It is only sufficient to give the order ! '

" ' But how do you stop them ? ' asked M. Loucheur.

" ' You know my plan,' replied Foch, ' I simply place

a stickfast here and another there and the Boches can go no further.'

"The English conference being ended, the Anglo-French conference began. M. Poincaré spoke first. He explained the situation and added that for him there was no question of stopping the Boches anywhere except where they were then and not elsewhere.

"Sir Douglas Haig said that for his part he was prepared to do his best and defend Amiens.

"Marshal Foch sprang forward and cried, 'No! It is not a question of Amiens. We must first conquer where we are now!'

"In a few words he went on to urge that the Boches must be stopped at once, and for this it was sufficient to give the order.

"At this moment Lord Milner rose and signed to M. Clemenceau, to whom he repeatedly said, 'There is the man!'

"Sir Douglas also rose and joined Lord Milner and M. Clemenceau. Sir Douglas Haig energetically pleaded in favour of a single command.

"'We have our only remedy,' he said, 'and that is to put over me and over Pétain a chief to whom we will both be responsible. As for me, I would willingly place myself under the orders of Foch. I had already telegraphed this to my Government 48 hours ago.'

"M. Clemenceau returned to the table and in a loud voice proposed to General Pétain to do the same as Sir Douglas Haig and place himself under the orders of Foch.

"The declaration was then drawn up appointing Foch Commander-in-Chief."

.   .   .   .   .   .

We moved on through Doullens; who should we pass on the road outside but Toc 5, who had left us at Grévillers.

We halted for a few minutes at the Mézerolles road corner to wait for the officers who had gone on ahead to arrange the billets. There was an estaminet beside us where I ate a feast the like of which I had never expected to taste again—coffee and omelettes, beaucoup omelettes !

We then turned down the hill into Mézerolles, a delightful little village lying a quarter-of-a-mile to the left of the main road and well below it. It straggled, but not unpleasantly like the villages of Artois. It possessed all the qualifications of a village in Arcady ; a rambling stream, an old stone bridge, a quaint little church, a twisting main street, a gay Mairie, a well stocked estaminet and, at the far end, it ran into a wooded hill and suddenly stopped, as though surprised at its audacity.

We billeted ourselves in the end farm just under the hill. Gardiner ran out lines to the houses where the Batteries had billeted themselves and for the next 48 hours the wires buzzed not with such messages as " S.O.S. Left Division", or " Fire 30 rounds at Bapaume Station", but " How many greatcoats are you deficient of ? " or " Reply at once to my wire re number of lorries out of action".

Toc 2—of course—established a firm liaison with the Squadron who had fixed up a temporary landing ground near by. The Squadron listened enviously to tales of the Bapaume Canteen and many boxes of cigars were bartered for " flips " over the line. The R.F.C. were all simply magnificent ; during the crisis every pilot and observer flew practically continuously from dawn to dusk.

We slept, cleaned ourselves, and examined our wounds. We had only lost one how. out of 22—the one which Toc 2 had ditched in the shell hole at Maricourt Wood on March 21st. The how. abandoned by Toc 1 had been found and salved by one of the horse-drawn batteries of our old friends, 48th Brigade R.G.A. In addition, Toc 1 had lost one nine-two barrel which had toppled into the Ancre while crossing Miraumont Bridge—hence probably the report that the bridge at Achiet-le-Grand was down! The A.S.C. subaltern in charge of the move had almost managed to fish it out again when the Boche appeared on the skyline so he had to abandon it. Five months later, when we advanced again, the Major of Toc 1 made a bee line for Miraumont Bridge, but the barrel had gone—perhaps to adorn the Tiergarten in Berlin.

Considering the severity of the fighting, our casualties had been wonderfully light : 12 killed, 43 wounded and one or two missing—but this does not include casualties inflicted by the 9.45 which burst amongst the reinforcements. Our losses in gun stores and kit were great but the firm which employed us was a big one and was soon able to make them good (though the magic words " Lost in the retreat " served so frequently that at last a G.R.O.* was published forbidding them !)

On the morning of the second day at Mézerolles the Major of Toc 1 came round to complain bitterly about being out of the Battle. He craved permission to go off on a roving commission with one Four-Wheel-Drive carrying thirty rounds of ammunition and towing one how. but the Colonel, after consultation with Corps Heavies, refused ; infantry and field artillery were to have sole use of the roads at present.

The same afternoon a car went along the Doullens road, where the Major of Toc 4 happened to be inspecting

* General Routine Order.

his hows., and a Staff Officer leant out and cried hysterically :

" What are all these guns doing back here ? They ought to be in the line ! "

We wondered if he were one of the same Staff Officers who had taken Toc 1's ammunition lorry.

In the evening the welcome orders arrived that on the following morning the Brigade was to reconnoitre for Battery positions in the Bertrancourt area and hold itself in readiness to move into action at an hour's notice.

MARCH 28TH, 1918

Early next morning the Colonel and the Majors and I drove back towards the line. Doullens was packed; the New Zealand Division was detraining at the Station. Doullens itself was recovering fast, already the shops were re-opening and prices were soaring; it was said a French Division would arrive shortly.

The Doullens-Acheux road was almost empty; things seemed to be settling down splendidly. Marieux Château, the lovely home of Corps Headquarters, was a centre of reassuring activity. From Authie to Bus we drove through budding woods. Battalions of big New Zealanders resting by the roadside cursed us savagely as we spattered them with mud. Chinks were hard at work digging reserve lines which were never used.

Bus was full; interpreters belonging to the New Zealand Division were hurrying about with note-books in their hands searching garrulously for billets for the Divisional Trench Mortars, for the Divisional Supply Company, for the A.P.M., the C.R.E., the Ordnance, and a dozen more. Officers were seeking sites for the Salvage Dump, for the Divisional Canteen, and for the Prisoner-of-War cage. The Château had just been taken over for Divisional Headquarters; it would not be easy to find a billet anywhere in Bus so we drove on. Joy of joys, at the Colincamps corner there actually stood a New Zealand Military Policeman as smart as if there wasn't a Boche within fifty miles.

"No," said he, "you can't go along the Colincamps Road. The diggers have only just driven the Boche out and they're working forward to Mailly-Maillet now."

So we went to Bertrancourt instead where the Colonel left me to find a billet for Brigade Headquarters and pushed on towards Beaussart with the Majors to look for Battery positions. But Bertrancourt was hopelessly full of infantry and Maori pioneers and wagon lines so I walked back through the mud to Bus and told the first interpreter I saw that we were the Heavy Artillery attached to his Division and that we *must* find a headquarters somewhere in Bus.

"No; sorry," he said. "Eet is impossible, full up!"

"But the Divisional Commander will be angry if the Heavy Artillery attached to his Division is unable to find a billet!"

"Well," said he coldly, "I will see what can be done; for instance try Billet No. 32."

But Billet No. 32 was impossibly small and dirty.

"No!" said I firmly, "I cannot ask the Commander of a Heavy Artillery Brigade to live in such a hole."

The interpreter was visibly impressed. "Is eet for the Commander of a Heavy Artillery Brigade himself that you seek a billet?" he asked.

I nodded gravely.

"Well," said he, "I think that Billet No. 91 will suit your General admirably. Would you care for me to lead your there?"

So off we went together to Billet No. 91; a charming, low, red-roofed house with a big garden in front, where I made the acquaintance of Monsieur, a nice old schoolmaster; of Mathilde, his shrewish wife; and of Jeanette, their graceful and pretty daughter.

"Yes," I told the interpreter, "this will suit us admirably; the General will be very pleased. I would like that big room for his bedroom and—if it would not inconvenience Madame—that small room beside it for the office and mess, also the cellar for the telephone exchange."

"No!" protested Madame, "The cellar is impossible —the cider and the potatoes!"

"Ca ne fait rien, Mathilde," interposed Monsieur gently.

But Madame was adamant—at least until the interpreter had spoken rapidly to her for five minutes about *La France* and *Réquisitions* and such like. Monsieur stood by and nodded approvingly while Jeanette winked at me and smiled and pouted and pirouetted on her toes.

In the end we all sealed the bargain with a bottle of Graves and I walked back through the mud to Bertrancourt to meet the Colonel. We drove back to Mézerolles where we loaded our lorries and next morning—

MARCH 29TH, 1918

—we all moved back to the war again, to the excitement of crowds of waving children and tearful old women. In Doullens the King drove past us.

And there let us stop—though I could write much more about how the New Zealanders and the 42nd Division and others held the Boche impotently pinned to the marshes of the Ancre until such time as they saw fit to drive him back sixty miles through Bapaume and Le Quesnoy to the Mormal Forest. And how Toc 1 came back to the very same position that they had occupied early in 1916 when they first arrived from England; how Toc 2 " won " a piano (and—more wonderful still—kept it); how Toc 3 went through the mill again down by the Mailly-Maillet corner; how Toc 4 shot up a Boche " sausage " that was being hauled along the Miraumont Road; and how Toc 5 returned to us and finally left us for another Brigade, but not before they turned the Colonel's hair grey by dropping their shells 6000 yards short.

And how Major Austin swore that he could distinctly see a Boche camp from Tusculum Redivivum; how he took it on and claimed a direct hit on a tent at a range of 12,000 yards; how Corps Heavies believed him (and we didn't); and how the press correspondents swallowed it and telegraphed it home, where it appeared in all the papers.

And how the Yanks at last really and truly arrived in the flesh and how the Hindenburg Line was broken and how I re-visited my old dug-out at Beugny and found it filled with a blackening heap of German dead.

And how gallant Hatch was killed and how Aglionby left us to command a Battery of his own—to be killed up in Flanders by a trench mortar bomb while reconnoitring for a forward battery position, but not before he had won a Military Cross—and how we entered Le Quesnoy and how the Colonel had a narrow escape there and how the Divisional Commander of the New Zealand Division wrote him a farewell letter of which we were so proud that I must print it in full:—

"All good things come to an end and amongst others the association of the New Zealand Division with the IV Corps and consequently the 90th Brigade.

"It has been, as times go, a long partnership and a successful one. We shall carry away with us none but pleasant memories and sincere admiration for the work done by you and your Brigade.

"I do not know how it came about, but we have had closer personal touch and more confidence in you and your guns than at any time since the Division has been in France.

"I hope you will let your men know this and that this expression on my part is not merely a courtesy as between one unit and another but the feeling of every man in the ranks."

And I should like to tell you about Jimmy and Billy and Buck and Blinky and Old Bill and "Hammersly"; and how ammunition-carrying Tanks were attached to us and how Toc 3 won a Croix de Guerre and two M.Cs. and how the Colonel added a C.M.G. to his D.S.O. and how 2nd Lieut. —— of Toc — did *not* get either. And how Gilly disposed of the Triumph I borrowed at Achiet-le-Grand when an annoying order came out calling for the engine numbers of all motor-cycles in the possession of units; how the Doc proudly left us in May " to return to Harley Street " but how he didn't get beyond a hospital in Aldershot ; how Benwell carried on for weeks though suffering from appendicitis ; how Gardiner nearly got the sack because he never could get up in the morning ; how we celebrated the Armistice ; how Edwards of Toc 3 nearly blew us up with his home-made fireworks ; and how the Colonel, disconsolate at having nothing to do, started an accursed salvage dump. . . .

. . . . . .

Most of this I have written in my office in the big Demobilisation Camp where it is my fate to work. Now and then lorries rumble past my door—great, dusty, companionable creatures with their friendly purr : occasionally even a Vauxhall glides sweetly and swiftly by.

And then I remember and I wistfully long for the days that have gone. I have forgotten the destruction of the Field Ambulance, the shell that burst amongst the reinforcements, the bitter dawn when we heard that the enemy had broken through at Mory.

I can only remember the joys of the Bapaume Canteen, that mad moonlight drive, the magic bagpipes of the 51st Division, the glow of confidence I felt when I saw the splendid big New Zealanders detraining at Doullens. But those days have gone, never to return. . . .

Alas, the 90th Brigade is now nothing more than a memory ; its Colonel is shooting wild duck in Norfolk, its Doctor is in America, its Orderly Officer is in a London bank, its Sergeant-Major is in India, its batteries have vanished like ripples in the water ; only the trail of its graves remains.

Summer, 1919.

Aglionby wrote the following account of his share in the fighting of the Nine Days. Through the kindness of his parents I am able to give it in full :—

AGLIONBY'S ACCOUNT.

MARCH 21ST.

About 5 a.m. I was wakened up by a very heavy gas and high explosive barrage in our valley. I got up, dressed, and put my gas mask on. Mitchell and Swaine came in and I sent them to warn everyone on that side of the valley to put their masks on. Then I went over to the B.C. Post.

It was very dark and though I had a torch I did not know exactly where I was when I got to the road the other side of the valley. The gas shells made so much noise that one could not hear the H.E. burst unless they were almost on top of one. I was afraid I should get in front of No. 2 gun just as they were going to fire. I found a shelter with a light but it was empty. Then I got on the road but got off again as a shell burst very near and I thought I should be safer under the bank. I nearly ran into another just after that and then I made out the wireless mast and so found the B.C. Post.

Graham was up and we waited a few minutes and then Callis came in and we got two guns firing—Graham going to the left section, Callis and I to the right. We went on till dawn when the barrage ceased, though one big fellow was shelling just behind No. 6 pit very consistently and others were dropping

Hugh Aglionby.

AGLIONBY'S ACCOUNT

intermittently all over the position. We all felt better when we got our masks off, mine having hurt the side of my head so that I had to take it off every now and then to ease it, while still of course breathing through it.

About 8 I had breakfast got for the men and went over to the mess with Callis for breakfast. He was then shelling the Decauville* beyond No. 1 pit and then started on the bank above; we went back to the B.C. post and took the papers and maps down the sap. I sent Michell off to the rear position and Timmis to Brigade—all lines having been down since the start. The rest of the forenoon passed without incident; we gathered from wounded officers and men that the Boche was in our front line and, in places, in the support. This did not sound too bad, and I sent a runner to Brigade and had lunch. I had just finished and was lighting a cigar when Peggs, one of the servants, pointed out a number of men on the sky line.

The battery position was in a valley running roughly east and west, with other valleys running out of it to the north. Just in front of the guns a valley ran off towards Vaulx, then came the Morchies-Vaulx road, then Maricourt Wood—most of the trees of which had been cut down but a lot of undergrowth remained. About 1000 yards past the Wood the valley makes a bend to the right and, passing through Lagnicourt, joins the Agache Valley at Quéant. Just before it reaches Lagnicourt a wider valley runs north towards Vaulx and Noreuil. The far side of this valley, which we knew as the Burton Ridge (from the O.P. on it), is the sky line from the Battery as one looks up the valley.

* Light railway track.

It was on the Burton Ridge, then, that we saw large numbers of men running about but I could not be certain that they were Germans.

It was about 2 p.m. when we made up our minds that they were Germans, being assisted by a Sapper Captain who reported the enemy considerably nearer. We accordingly opened fire. The Germans were then standing or running about in groups; when we fired at them they moved off in the direction of Noreuil and stopped hanging about the valley.

Then we got a written message from Callis, who had gone up to Luke O.P. (about 1000 yards to our left front) shortly after breakfast, that there were massed Germans coming over our old front line. We fired at them till things in the valley began to demand our attention again. The Boche were now coming up in our direction on the north slope and I could see a wave of them come up to some wire in front of the Morchies-Noreuil road. Accordingly I turned all guns on to them and, when they had gone, fired at some more who had come up into the valley. I was sitting on the curved iron roof of the officers' mess cook-house shouting corrections across the valley to the B.C. post. A machine-gun opened fire on me and for the rest of the afternoon I sat behind the roof and looked over the top.

I was getting very anxious about Callis at the O.P. as the enemy seemed spreading very quickly round the country and I could not see any sign of infantry coming up, while a number of our own men were coming back through the Battery. I had already posted my surplus gunners in the defence positions round our two machine-gun posts (as we had previously settled); they went to their posts quickly and without confusion. I rallied such of our infantry as I had time to stop and posted them in shell holes but there were no officers and, until I could detail one of mine for the job, they mostly drifted away. Much to my relief, Callis turned up shortly afterwards and stayed with me on the kitchen roof. He said that the enemy were not far off the Brown Line and that he had been driven from the O.P. by machine-gun fire.

The enemy were now up the hill and through the wire into the Morchies-Noreuil road, where it is sunken. We could not stop them from getting there but we prevented them coming farther and, after two shells had pitched in the road, the whole lot of them ran back towards Lagnicourt—a very encouraging sight. We lengthened our range and followed them over the crest ; it was some time before any came back.

In the meantime another force of Boche had appeared at the bottom of the valley and were coming on very fast. We got on to them but they were in little parties of five or six and a good many of them got through into the dead ground. Their supports, however, did not like the look of it and turned up the hill into the sunken road. About this time a field gun was brought up to within 1500 yards of us and started firing at us. They put one through the camouflage of No. 3 gun and several went very close above our heads. I could see the flash quite clearly and thought I could see the observer. We fired at the cross roads at the bottom of the valley and must have hit the gun or its ammunition, for we heard no more of it.

Of the enemy who came through our fire I only saw one patrol of three men just to the left of Maricourt Wood, and some 500 yards in front of the Battery. We did not use our Lewis guns on them as I made up my mind to stick to the defence scheme we had previously evolved and not disclose the fact that we had machine-guns until the Boche were just in front of our battery wire. For the rest of the afternoon, while the light lasted, we went on firing at the Boche whenever we saw him.

I do not remember the exact order in which things happened but they were all a repetition of what had gone before. There was a big crowd of men standing on the top of Burton Ridge, near the O.P., and we started ranging on them but before we got there we had to drop on to some others in the neighbourhood of the sunken road. We afterwards got back to the former and drove them off the ridge.

About 5.30 p.m. some infantry came up from Beugny to rescue some of our men who were cut off near Lagnicourt on our right front. I told them what I knew of the situation and helped them by firing at the cross roads in the valley. These were the only infantry we saw coming up from Beugny.

It was now getting dark and the situation was far from clear. All the afternoon I had been acting on the assumption that our supports were coming up from Vaulx —this had been verified by reports from infantry, and I had myself seen some of them. I had therefore tried to turn the enemy northwards to get them caught but I did not know how far south our infantry had come or whether—if they were in front of us—they were likely to hold if attacked. I had therefore already sent Graham to Brigade telling him to report that I could not hold the position if attacked at night and that at the same time it would be very difficult to move the guns. (We were 800 yards from the nearest point that could be reached by lorries; the General had previously agreed that we could not move without horses.)

We waited in the sap as, if the Boche started his barrage again, I did not want to have to recross the valley in the dark. It was now very dark: no shelling and no machine-gun fire.

Graham returned with orders for us to stay but was followed with an order for us to move to Fremicourt. The Colonel wrote he could get no horses. I had tried to borrow a team from 156 Heavy Battery but they said that all their horses were away and were not expected to return that night. Accordingly I sent word to Brigade that I could not move without horses and that I could not get any.

The men had had a long and tiring day; for the last three weeks we had been shooting night and day, besides sending big fatigue parties to make reserve positions. The men had not had two consecutive nights in bed for a month.

The Colonel sent back word that we must do our utmost to move. Accordingly I got all the guns out of their pits and sent Sergeant-Major Dowling to pull No. 3 gun along the Decauville—the valley having so many new shell holes and being so cut by the transport that I thought we had a better chance that way. He got it half-way and stuck. Just then I heard that 156 Heavy Battery had got horses and I sent Smith to try and borrow them, which he did. Luckily the Boche was hardly firing at all. I waited till the first gun had been got up to the road and then went off to find the new position with Callis and Graham. We got there about 1 a.m. and found billets for the men.

The guns came in singly from the forward position.

No. 6 had fallen into a shell hole and the combined efforts of the team of horses and all the available men could not get it out. We got a little uncomfortable rest, I on someone's kit-bag.

MARCH 22ND.

Next morning we took the Officers' Club as a mess and started making the position presentable. We also made arrangements to take a team of horses back to Maricourt Wood to salve the gun and the rest of the stores after dark. We were firing hard most of the morning but could not see anything from where we were. The Boche shelled the area slightly and was apparently attacking Vaulx.

After lunch I was sent for by Brigade and ordered to select a new position at Avesnes (behind Bapaume), and move into it at once. I took Callis and went on ahead to choose it; we found quite a good spot away from any definite landmark and close to a road. We went back and found the Battery packing up and one gun still firing. The lorries we expected had not come so I had the ammunition and stores collected by the roadside and the guns sent on ahead.

The Boche was shelling the other end of the village. I was rather doubtful about the lorries turning up, but they did before the barrage lifted on to our end of the village.

Callis and I went back to the new position and got dug-outs for the men, fine bomb-proof ones made by the R.O.D.*

The B.C. post we put in a large dug-out used by the Expeditionary Force Canteen people at the adjoining canteen.

* Railway Operating Department.

The guns and the stores came up all right but we were not allowed to send back to Maricourt Wood for our other gun and so we had to leave it. The sight had been taken away and we had done the breech block in, however. We were all glad to get a night's rest and turned in early.

MARCH 23RD.

At 5 a.m. a message came from the Colonel that the Boche was through on the left and had reached Sapignies (about 2000 yards to our left front). Battery Commanders were to act on their own responsibility. I got the men out and looked over the valley to Sapignies but could see no sign of the Boche, though there was certainly firing just over the crest. An infantry battalion was resting by the road and I had a long talk with their Colonel but he knew very little. We afterwards heard it was a false alarm.

We got breakfast for the men and trained the guns on the crest. I also found an ammunition dump and got up as much as possible. About 8.30 a.m. we started firing and got a line through to Brigade. The Colonel said the Boche was coming on and he thought we were all for it. We had had our Lewis guns posted and kept two guns trained on the crest until I felt sure from what I could see of the behaviour of people near Sapignies that the Boche advance had been magnified.

We did a lot of firing that day but what made most impression on us was that the Canteen had been abandoned by its staff, and was in our charge. There were hundreds of cases of whisky and beer, besides groceries, in three large marquees. I put a guard on the liquor as I was afraid of a riot if it was broached, and let the men take what groceries they wanted. Men from all quarters came flocking in and a good deal of stuff was wasted so I had the place cleared and ordered the stuff to be issued to units only, and no spirits without my signature.

The Canteen successfully solved the ration problem and did a lot to cheer up our gunners who went about for days afterwards smoking Coronas. I found a cricket bat and ball and took them down to the mess and started a cricket team, although we did not get so far as playing. By the evening the Boche on the left appeared to be held. He did a certain amount of shelling round us but justified our selection of the position by doing most of it on the wood to our immediate right.

MARCH 24TH.

After a quiet night we spent much the same sort of morning as on the previous day but in the afternoon were ordered to move to Achiet-le-Petit. The big dump on the Bapaume-Arras road went up just as we were going and made a tremendous noise. The guns went first ; the men had to march. Unfortunately some of the lorries broke down en route and at one time we had no fewer than three distinct parties on the road beside the foot sloggers. The lorries also got sent the wrong way by the A.S.C. and I spent a hectic afternoon on a motor bike keeping in touch with all of them. The men arrived about dusk but the guns did not arrive till some time later. There was no cover or accommodation so about 8 p.m. I sent the guns on to Logeast Wood with orders to park and await my return while I went off to meet the Colonel at 40th Divisional Headquarters.

We missed the Colonel but the General told us what he wanted us to do. We met the Colonel on the way back and he insisted on an immediate reconnaissance

AGLIONBY'S ACCOUNT

in his car. We went first to Logeast where I found that my guns had got in, then on to Achiet-le-Grand and Courcelles. The Boche started shelling the road and we came back.

I found that the infantry had taken all the accommodation so I went straight to their Brigadier and got all the huts I wanted. I then went to bed but was roused after about an hour by the Adjutant who had fresh orders from the Division.

Some time after he left, two officers of an infantry battalion came in and said they thought I might like to know that their line of outposts (which they seemed to think was the front line) ran just behind our guns! They said their Colonel was at the cross roads and would see me if I wished. I was suspicious and went to the Brigadier who said the two officers were wrong. I then spent about half-an-hour looking for them but could not find them so went back to bed.

MARCH 25TH.

Next morning after breakfast I chose a position in Logeast Wood and sent the guns up to it. Then the Infantry Brigadier came along and wanted us to fire on Sapignies so we rushed two guns back along the road and came straight into action. In the meantime Stokoe turned up from Division where he had been acting as liaison officer for the Brigade. I spent the rest of the morning between the Battery and Infantry Brigade Headquarters. The Boche did not appear to be advancing in their sector.

About mid-day the Field Artillery came back through Logeast Wood and I heard from other batteries in the Brigade that we were all to go to Acheux, about 15 miles further back.

Infantry came back past the guns saying the Boche were coming on but the Infantry Brigadier, who rode past at the moment, said he did not think it was so.

I offered to stay as long as I had ammunition if he wanted me to do so, but he said I had better get on to Acheux.

We had got the men and guns separated by about 500 yards; the cooks had just got the dinner ready so I had the men at the rear guns fallen in and marched up to the forward guns, where the food was, and then fell them out for dinner. There was a good deal of transport and some infantry hurrying down the roads.

In the meantime some tanks appeared on our left rear and said that the Boche were in Achiet-le-Grand (under a mile away) and that they themselves were going to cover the retreat. Some machine-gunners appeared and started digging furiously just beside us.

I thought it was time to be off but, as we had a long way to go over very congested roads and as most of the men would have to march, I thought it would have a steadying effect if we did everything in a leisurely fashion. I could not see any Boche in front and we had a tank on the left which I hoped might do something to keep the men together. So we fell in by sections, told off the new men into their right places, and pushed off. Graham, Stokoe and I went on in the car to find out the route and get billets. The Boche were shelling the entrance of Ablainzeville when we went through. I did not like the idea of the battery coming through and was going back when we saw a big block in the traffic ahead. As there were no signs of it clearing I thought we had better straighten it out before the guns arrived in case the Boche shelled up and down the road. The traffic was in an awful mess, double banked all the way, and carts

AGLIONBY'S ACCOUNT

and G.S. wagons were squeezing in from both sides whenever they got the chance. The real trouble was about half-a-mile up, where the road ran into another which was also overcrowded with transport.

I left Stokoe and Graham to keep anything else from getting on the road and went to the cross roads, where I acted as traffic control, taking care to let our road have its full share.

The guns got through the village all right and Michell had taken the men round. We got through Bucquoy and went on to Puisieux where we halted and changed the men on the lorries.

Then I went on to Acheux, telling the Battery to wait up a side road near Mailly-Maillet until I came back, as the lorries were running out of petrol. I found Brigade and, after scrounging 30 gallons of petrol, I went back to the Battery which was at the rendezvous having tea.

We went on again at once as I knew the Boche were not far off and Graham and I went off to Louvencourt and got billets for the men.

They all arrived without mishap, and next day (MARCH 26TH) we marched another 15 miles to Mézerolles, Graham and I again going on to get billets.

. . . .

I was much impressed with the behaviour of both officers and men during these six days. There was never any confusion and everyone did exactly as he was told as if he was in absolutely normal conditions. As far as I know no one missed a meal and we had good quarters for the men whenever we were not actually moving. Not a man was lost on any march although the roads were crowded and we were often split up.

(*It is hard to understand why Aglionby did not receive the D.S.O. for which he was recommended.*)

Final History of the Brigade
FROM APRIL, 1918.

During the summer months of 1918 we played our part in the bitter and tiring fighting which, in little more than a hundred days, established a definite and complete ascendency over the enemy.

In July we moved out to Pas for a week's rest ; while we were there we were most successfully inspected by the Army Commander himself, General Byng. You musn't repeat it but it was he who, trying in vain to look down the barrel of a six-inch how., whispered to a subaltern of Toc 4, " How on earth d'you open the door ? "

August 21st, the opening day of the final Allied offensive, found us still with the Fourth Corps, attacking Bucquoy, Fonquevillers and Hébuterne in support of the 5th Division (recently returned from Italy), the 37th Division, the 42nd (East Lancashire) Division and the New Zealand Division.

We were with the New Zealanders when they recaptured Bapaume a few days later and in two wonderful months we advanced some thirty miles via Ruyaulcourt, Bethencourt, Briastre (where poor Hatch was killed by a shell that struck him in the back) to Salesches, a wretched village just west of the walled and moated town of Le Quesnoy, which was dramatically stormed by the New Zealanders on November 4th. It is worthy of note that we claimed for the Brigade car the honour of being the first Allied car to enter Le Quesnoy—it is also worthy of note that it was in Le Quesnoy that the Colonel was nearly kissed by a grateful old woman (but you musn't repeat that either).

A day or two before the Armistice, the Divisions of the IV Corps drove the Boche right out of Mormal Forest ; the roads were so bad that for the first time in our existence we were unable to follow up.*

Thus it was that the 11th November found us still at Salesches, ten miles or more behind the Infantry and probably twenty from the nearest Boche. A small group of officers assembled outside the Adjutant's office and greeted 11 o'clock with a hollow cheer.

At Salesches we stayed until we knew every smell by heart ; we had no whisky, no beer, no cigarettes. . . .

A week or so before Christmas we sadly said good-bye to Toc 1 (whom we were to leave behind) and trekked forward by road via Le Quesnoy, Bavai, Maubeuge and Mons to Genappe, a pleasing town midway between Brussels and Charleroi. Here it was that demobilisation set in and the Adjutant contrived to be the first of the officers to go home. Graham, the Orderly Officer, reigned in his stead.

During the three months the Brigade stayed at Genappe, so much hospitality was thrust upon it that it almost—but not quite—made up for not being able to go home. In April the Brigade—or what was left of it—moved by easy stages to Godesberg, the Maidenhead of Cologne.

* Toc 2 sent forward two hows. and were in action in the heart of the Mormal Forest on November 6th and 7th. The Colonel himself helped to haul into position No. 2 gun, the last of the Brigade's pieces to fire a round in the War. Toc 2 were unable to advance any further owing to the destruction of the bridges over the Sambre.

There the 90th Brigade faded away so rapidly that a few weeks later it died at the early age of two—but not without, I think, having amply justified its existence.

It was survived by its father, Lieut.-Colonel A. H. Thorp, C.M.G., D.S.O., R.G.A.—its mother, Regimental-Sergeant-Major J. H. Oatley, Médaille Militaire, had deserted it at Genappe.

.   .   .   .   .   .

Since then three events of Brigade interest have occurred. Two successful Reunion Dinners have been held in London and the Colonel, after half a-century of Bachelorhood, has become a Benedict!

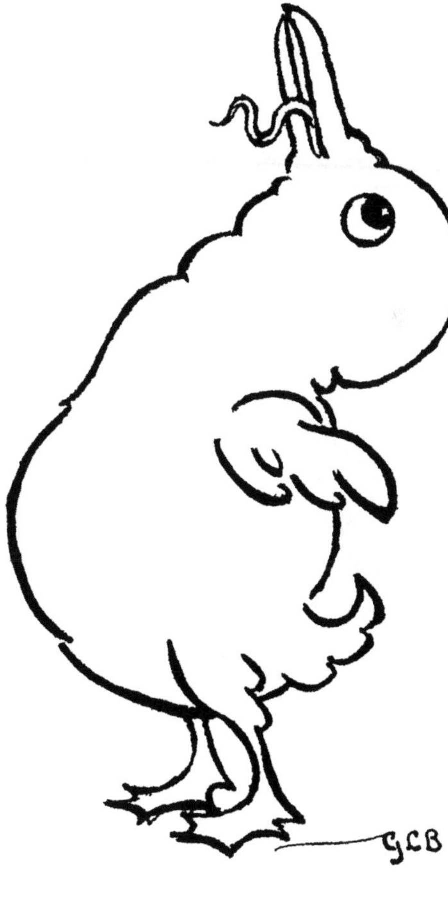
GLB

Appendix

THE STORY OF HOW TOC 1 LOST A PIECE AT MIRAUMONT BRIDGE.

By Lieut. G. T. L. Macartney, R.A.S.C.

(See page 72.)

Each nine-two, when dismantled for travelling, packs on to three transporting-carriages, which are then coupled together and drawn by a "Cat".

Owing to Toc 1's guns being somewhat incomplete, we had to improvise couplings out of chains and tow ropes; this meant that the two rear transporting-carriages were wobbling about and not following in the tracks of the front one.

On March 22nd Ticehurst (the junior A.S.C. officer of Toc 1) came to me and reported that they had been in difficulties at Miraumont Bridge and that, owing to the improvised couplings, a carriage containing one of the "pieces" (technical term for gun-barrel) had run over the side of the bridge. The bridge was very shaky and dangerous and there were a lot of troops of all sorts coming down the road in retreat. They had tried to pull the carriage back on the bridge, but the chains broke and it fell into the river.

Early next morning I went to have a look at it and found that it was upside down in the middle of the stream with its wheels up in the air. The river bank at this point was about three feet high; the muzzle of the piece was right up against it. I saw from the first it was a gamble whether I could save it or not, but decided to have a try. Accordingly I went back to Siege Park and brought up two " Cats " belonging to an 8-inch how. battery that had lost all its guns.

At first we found the bank too steep ; we started to dig it away on a slant. We dug at this all day but found it was of no use as when we hitched on the two " Cats " the piece only moved a few inches. During the afternoon we were intermittently shelled by a big high velocity gun which was probably shooting at the Railway Embankment close by. We returned to Siege Park just before dark.

During the night I thought out a plan and decided I could save it with a " gin " (special form of heavy lifting tackle), with which I could have lifted the whole thing clear of the bank and, with the help of a " Cat ", righted it on its wheels.

At dawn on the 24th I therefore set out in a lorry in search of Ordnance Workshops who, I heard, had moved to Mailly-Maillet. I went there but found no signs of them and was told that they had gone on to Sailly, a village north of Courcelles. I found them there and asked them for a gin but, owing to the confusion of the retreat, they couldn't find one. As it was then about noon I decided that the only thing to do was to return to Miraumont Bridge and render the piece useless.

With great difficulty I returned, meeting very heavy traffic all the way, and tried in vain to remove the breech block. In the end I took off the wheels, brakes, and winding chains of the carriage and returned to Siege Park. During the time we were working we were again shelled.

APPENDIX

Next morning (the 25th) I got hold of a couple of Gunners and A.S.C. men and went back to the Bridge to make another attempt to remove the breech block, but we were again heavily handicapped through lack of the proper tools. While making this final effort we heard that the enemy were in Achiet-le-Petit; by this time our infantry were retreating fast and, on seeing some of them come over the near crest in open order and put a machine-gun into position a couple of hundred yards away, we decided it was high time to clear out.

The following, collected from various sources, throw additional light on the events of the Nine Days :—

FROM ENEMY SOURCES.

Extracts from an unposted letter, written at Puisieux early in April by a Sergeant-Major of the 46th Infantry Regiment :—

"We had great confidence in our artillery. The guns, which included German, Austrian and captured guns from Russia, stood almost on top of one another. The Quéant-Pronville area was full of batteries which had been put in position some days before. The crews for many of these only arrived on the night of the 20th.

"At 5.30 a.m. the bombardment started, gas being fired on the enemy artillery. At 9 a.m. there was a pause in the firing so that the Tommies should come out of their positions: ten minutes later it commenced again on their trenches and at ten o'clock we attacked. At 10.15 we were already in their trenches and the 58th Division in the enemy second line. The few Scotsmen remaining alive were taken prisoners and sent to the rear, their cigarettes being first taken from them. We had by this time several casualties. In the evening we were in possession of Doignies where we captured several guns. . . .

"Owing to the rain the roads are half a metre deep in mud. The horses are dying like flies; I counted 37 on a stretch of road 4 kilometres long, the majority having been killed by artillery fire."

A prisoner of the same regiment, captured near Bucquoy on April 5th, stated :—

"On the 21st British Heavy Artillery obtained a direct hit on the Regimental Battle Headquarters of the 58th Infantry Regiment near Boursies, killing 5 officers (including the Regimental Commander) and several men."

A Dug-Out in a German Battery Position Destroyed by 90 Brigade R.G.A.

APPENDIX

Notes on a lecture delivered on March 18th, taken from the diary of an officer of the 119th Grenadier Regiment:—

"The direction of the main attack is due West towards the coast, Abbeville, and Boulogne, with the intention of separating the English from the French; the blow to be delivered chiefly against the former. The plans are so thorough that failure is impossible: if the attack fails in one place it is to be broken off and another place tried."

Extracts from the diary of a dead officer of the 73rd Fusilier Regiment:—

"20.4.18. We had indented for a car the day before from Group and so we set out in the direction of Mory. The run through the country recently regained was interesting. Quéant, for a start, left a disconsolate impression although everything had already been neatly tidied up and the Tommies were already working hard on improving the roads. The sight of the prisoners was rather depressing. War-weary and dejected, no more of that supercilious, haughty bearing as last year after the battle of the Somme. . . . Thus war has changed a smiling country-side into a desert, and the only explanation I can find for the obstinacy of our enemies is that they believe all is lost.

"In the hottest hours of the day I walked to Bapaume whence the afternoon train leaves for Cambrai. What a sight the town is! A few gables were still standing, but otherwise there was nothing of a single house left. Tommy's camps outside the town look like negro villages in Central Africa. From Bapaume our road took us along the erstwhile English Lines of Communication. Tommy has laid out plenty of railroads for us and the rolling stock we captured renders us valuable service. Along the railway English ammunition was still lying in heaps. He had to leave all sorts of things behind. Prisoners were lending a hand to keep the track in repair."

FROM BRITISH SOURCES.

Information from an escaped prisoner of the 51st (Highland) Division :—

"At the commencement of the enemy offensive on March 21st, this private soldier was in a dug-out near the Bapaume-Cambrai road at Louverval. Gas was mixed with the first barrage and the British garrison kept underground. The enemy got round the left flank and rear of the position in great force, marching in artillery formation with complete companies, and overwhelmed all resistance. A very large number of German wounded were distributed all over the area north of Louverval and British prisoners were employed carrying them to dressing stations. The German wounded were very callously treated and bandages and dressings ran out. Between 10 a.m. and noon, field batteries were being brought into action north of Louverval near our old front line. Prisoners of war were taken to Denain *via* Cambrai, the hospitals on the way being packed and large numbers of walking wounded on the road. The traffic consisted entirely of horse-transport in poor condition drawn by Russian ponies and ill-fed horses. The roads were crowded but not blocked.

"A Prisoner-of-War Company was formed and employed on repairing the roads around Lagnicourt.

"This escaped private soldier acquired a German great coat; then, some days later, he hid in a cellar in Lagnicourt; found a German cap, gas-mask, and trousers; and made his way *via* Vaulx and Fremicourt to Bapaume. Hutments and villages were all occupied but the roads were nearly free from transport both by day and by night. The old C.C.S. at Grévillers was still used as such. He got past a control-post outside Bapaume by getting on to a tractor-drawn heavy gun and letting the driver do the talking, and passed all who accosted him by paying no attention.

"After a night in Bapaume, he proceeded *via* the railway into our lines near Puisieux."

HISTORIES OF THE BATTERIES.

TOC 1

By A. F. B.

(From information supplied by Sergeant T. B. Wilson, M.S.M.)

NINETY-FIVE SIEGE BATTERY R.G.A. was formed at Crosby, near Liverpool, in January 1916, of men of the Lancashire and Cheshire R.G.A. (T.F.), under the command of Captain Wheeler, a Lancashire and Cheshire officer.

The Battery moved to Horsham, trained there until it went overseas on May 25th, and, a week or two later, went into its first position at Bayencourt. It fought in the Battle of the Somme and advanced *via* Maricourt to Guillemont where Hatch joined the Battery and where, on November 10th, a chance shell struck the mess—a shack a couple of hundred yards behind the guns—and killed Wheeler and Paterson (another Lancashire and Cheshire officer) while they were at their breakfast.

Balfour, the only surviving Lancashire and Cheshire officer, became Major; the Battery moved from Guillemont to Hem, from Hem to Le Forest (where casualties were heavy), thence, early in '17, up north to the Vimy Ridge.

After the capture of the Ridge the Battery was ordered to the Salient and went into position in the gardens of the florid Goldfish Château, a few hundred yards behind Ypres.

From the Goldfish Château the Battery moved forward to St. Jean for the Third Battle of Ypres.

It was here that a dressing station to which Sergeant Wilson had taken a wounded gunner came in for a sudden burst of very heavy shelling. All the R.A.M.C. staff were knocked out so Wilson set to work to carry the wounded, of whom there were some twenty or thirty, into a dug-out. While he was doing this an R.A.M.C. Major arrived, complimented him, took his name in order to recommend him for a D.C.M.—and was killed five minutes later.

In late September the Battery left for the Third Army front, and went into a luxurious position at St. Léger where it created amusement and gained notoriety through the erratic shooting of its guns, which by this time were pretty well worn.

It was here that the Colonel and I first met Toc 1. The Battery, having stated it was much too short of men to provide a working party to dig positions urgently needed for an incoming group of batteries, was discovered by us to be hard at work constructing a tennis court for the use of the officers!

Ninety-five left us to go to Havrincourt Wood for the Battle of Cambrai and rejoined us permanently in December, going into a good position with deep gun-pits and comfortable dug-outs and shacks between Beugny and Morchies.

Just before Christmas disaster overtook them. I remember well how we at Brigade were sitting quietly at tea listening to Toc 1 finishing off a 300-round shoot when suddenly we heard a loud explosion followed by silence. A few minutes later Balfour rang up and told us that there had been a Premature. The Doc and I went straight over in the car and found a number of ambulances and a great crowd of cold-blooded

MAJOR LUSHINGTON.

MAJOR PARGITER.

APPENDIX

infantry sightseers standing in the road that ran behind the guns. Number 4 gun and its entire detachment had been blown to pieces.

The cause of the Premature was never discovered ; some said that it was due to a faulty shell, others to road-grit which had never been cleaned off and which, the moment the gun fired, exerted so much pressure that the sides of the shell gave way and it exploded instantaneously.

A week or two later poor Balfour died of pneumonia in hospital at Grévillers while his Battery was passing through on its way to Gézaincourt. Harris temporarily took over command and the Battery was re-equipped with six beautiful nine-twos of the very latest mark, capable of shooting twelve thousand yards.

A day or two before the Battery returned to the line, it was joined by Major Pargiter—who had been severely wounded while serving with a Mountain Battery on the Indian Frontier.

Under his command Toc 1 reached a very high standard of efficiency and the only time I can remember that his Battery failed to find favour in the Colonel's eyes was the dreadful day, just before the Armistice, when the Colonel discovered that one of the guns had inadvertently been erected on top of a poor little telephone wire. Now the Colonel had a great passion for all things connected with telephones and to his mind telephone wire was absolutely sacred—anyone who saw a disused wire and failed to reel it in and treasure it for future occasions was outside the pale.

The Colonel, seething with fury, sent for the officer on duty and pointed to the wire, which had all but disappeared under the mud.

"What's that doing here?" he asked with difficulty, so great was his rage.

"Oh, it's only an old one: it's not in use, sir!" began Walker cheerfully.

It is an absolute fact that a party of New Zealanders working on the road a good fifty yards away downed tools and stopped work to listen to what the Colonel said to Walker.

. . . . . .

Immediately after the Retreat, Toc 1 went into position in the midst of a wilderness of railway sidings at Beaussart. Major Pargiter, who was returning to the Battery after a morning at the O.P., saw from afar a column of smoke rising from the sidings. He hastily telephoned through.

"Why on earth is that infernal engine standing there?" he cried. "Tell it to move on at once before it gives the position away."

Mournful laughter greeted him.

"That's not an engine, sir—it's the shed where all the officers' kit was!"

Curiously enough, this happened on the 1st of April.

. . . . . .

When we advanced into Belgium after the Armistice with our 6-inch how. Batteries, we had to leave Toc 1 behind: Major Pargiter went home—he is now a Brevet-Major with the British Military Mission in Lithuania—and his Battery finished its honourable career at Flesselles, near Amiens.

TOC 2

BY MAJOR F. LUSHINGTON, R.G.A.

TWO HUNDRED AND FORTY-FOUR SIEGE BATTERY R.G.A. came into being at Plymouth in September, 1916. In December it moved to Lydd for intensive training : thence, a month later, to Codford for mobilisation. On the night before the Battery sailed for France (January 28th) the War Office wired me to go down and take over command.

We crossed safely and landed at Havre, whence we went by rail and road to Dainville, near Arras.

For three weeks we were not allowed to go into action as our state of training was even worse than that of the average newly-formed battery of this period. Horton (my second-in-command) and myself were the only members of the Battery who had previously seen active service.

On March 5th we first went into action on the western outskirts of Arras, on the Arras-Dainville road : our state of training was still so low that either Horton or myself had to be on the guns day and night to superintend the smallest details—from the working out of the calculations to the actual laying of the sights and the fusing of the shells ! To make matters worse, our Battery-Quartermaster-Sergeant was so hopelessly at sea that he was almost incapable of finding us food and fuel—let alone " scrounging " luxuries. I mention these facts because it may interest future generations to know how men born and bred to the office stool, to the counter and the plough, found themselves suddenly hurled into the midst of primitive life, and accustomed themselves to it so quickly that within little more than a month they were fighting battles with the efficiency of hardened veterans.

At the end of March the Boche retreated to the Hindenburg Line : we moved forward into the Quarry at Achicourt. On April 8th, the eve of the Battle of Arras, Achicourt was very heavily shelled : the Battery came in for a good deal of it and behaved very well under its first experience of prolonged and concentrated shell-fire.

On April 9th, the opening day of the Battle of Arras, P. E. Thomas, an elderly subaltern, was killed in an O.P. at Beaurains (our first casualty), and a week later 2nd Lieut. C. Smith was killed by a shell that hit the mess.

On May 31st the Battery left the Arras front, having fought in all the actions of that Battle and having been in four different positions (Achicourt, Mercatel, Hénin, Hénin Hill). Our casualties up to now numbered about a dozen. Callis and Michell joined us in April and May respectively.

On June 1st the Battery went into action on the Ypres front in the garden of the Château des Trois Tours near Vlamertinghe : from this position we took part in the bombardment of the Battle of Messines.

On July 13th we were heavily shelled and had many casualties : from this date onward we were subjected to H.E. and gas-shell-fire daily and nightly. Stokoe, who joined us in July, was gassed ; Callis was also gassed. Two other officers were wounded, one left us with shell-shock, another with appendicitis. Four or five guns were knocked out : the office was destroyed twice and the mess three times.

APPENDIX 107

Finally, on the eve of the Third Battle of Ypres, we were ordered to move forward to Machine-Gun Farm, a quarter-of-a-mile ahead. Horton and myself were the only officers left : while two of my guns were on the road with Horton, an aeroplane called up the third one (which was still in action under my charge) for an important shoot. We had no wireless and no ground strips but the mess table-cloth was quickly torn up and, with the help of a telephone to the wireless at Group H.Q., a very successful shoot was carried out. At this period the Battery was at the top of the Army's weekly list of counter-battery shoots.

On July 31st the Third Battle of Ypres opened and the Battery moved forward to the Canal Bank, where Stokoe, who had just returned from hospital, was wounded in the arm. In August Horton left us to take command of a battery : Aglionby was posted to us to take his place. Graham joined us at the same time.

After moving forward twice more we received orders on September 30th to return to the Arras front.

During the three months that we had been in action in the Salient, we had sustained 90 casualties from gas and 60 from death, wounds, and sickness—out of a strength of 190. On only one occasion was the Battery actually put out of action—and then only for a few hours. This was the time when Aglionby and Callis had a marvellous escape : they were in a dug-out which was struck by an eight-inch shell ; everyone else in the dug-out was killed or wounded but they were untouched.

On October 2nd we came into action on the Arras-Tilloy road, next door to 299 Siege Battery, afterwards our sister-battery in 90 Brigade. On October 14th we took part in a big raid on the Monchy front : a few days later we moved to an exposed position on the Hénin-Croisilles road, where we remained a fortnight without firing a round. Timmis and Stobbart joined us here.

On November 27th, after the Battle of Cambrai, we went into action in the open fields between Beugny and Morchies: here we remained absolutely unshelled until the dawn of March 21st.

While we were in this position we found that with a little practice we could work out all calculations and turn a section of our guns on to any given target well inside three minutes—consequently we indulged in a good deal of sniping.

Early in December we joined 90 Brigade, and on Christmas Day and Boxing Day, with the snow lying thick on the ground, we carried out two long wire-cutting shoots. Russell, Smith and Pasifull joined us about this time.

In January (1918) I went up to IV Corps Heavy Artillery H.Q. as Acting Brigade-Major: the Battery went off to Gézaincourt for a fortnight's rest with the other batteries of the Brigade and returned to its position early in February, where the final month before the German offensive was chiefly spent in providing working parties for the Adjutant.

NOTE BY THE AUTHOR.—*Major Lushington stayed with his Battery until July 28th, 1918, when he was evacuated home with trench fever. Major M. R. Strover, D.S.O., took over command. Lushington returned to the Brigade a couple of months later and served with 299 Siege Battery until November 20th, when, owing to several changes, we were able to transfer him back to the command of 244 Siege Battery. He deserves special mention in that he was one of the few Battery Commanders who served practically continuously with his original Battery for two years.*

HARRAP (CROIX DE GUERRE). WORRALL (M.C.). MILLS (M.C.).

THREE OFFICERS OF TOC 3 WHO WON DECORATIONS.

APPENDIX

TOC 3

By Captain A. C. Mills, M.C., R.G.A.

Two Hundred and Seventy-Seven Siege Battery R.G.A. was formed at Weymouth in the late summer of 1916, under the command of Lieut. (afterwards Major) R. Sunley. In November the Battery moved to Aldershot for its training: Worrall and I joined it here.

After spending two cold and uncomfortable months at Aldershot, we moved to Lydd, where we were complimented for the smartness of our gun-drill and for our shooting on the ranges.

Three weeks later we went to Devizes to mobilise, and, after an unexpected couple of weeks delay owing to measles, we entrained for Southampton on March 21st, 1917, and sailed for Havre in the "Hunscraft"

On March 30th we went into a position in the fields near Dickebusch: on April 6th we fired our first round. We fought in the Battle of Messines and in the Third Battle of Ypres: our casualties were so heavy that, by the time we were transferred to the Third Army in October, only about twenty of the old hands were left.

We took part in the Battle of Cambrai, and joined 90 Brigade early in December. Major Sunley was wounded on March 21st; Major R. F. Burkitt, M.C., our next O.C., was wounded by a shell splinter a month or two later. Major H. E. Henderson, D.S.O., then took command and remained with us until the end of the War.

NOTE BY THE AUTHOR.—*277's total casualties during its twenty months of active service were some 70 killed and 120 wounded; of its original officers, Mills and Worrall alone were in at the death. Some 30 officers served with the Battery during its existence.*

TOC 4

BY MAJOR A. D. MCKILLOP CLARK, R.G.A.

TWO HUNDRED AND NINETY-NINE SIEGE BATTERY R.G.A. was formed in November, 1916, under the command of Major I. A. M. Cummins, R.G.A., at Fort Burgoyne, Dover. The Battery was trained at Horsham, Aldershot, and Lydd; mobilised at Larkhill in March, and landed in France on March 31st, 1917.

It first came into action at Kemmel, early in April, and took part in the Battle of Messines on the 5th and 6th of June. Thence the Battery went to the Ypres Sector, and was ordered to take up a position at Transport Farm, Zillebeke Lake, but was quickly strafed out and sent into position on the cross roads in Elverdinghe, close to the church. A fortnight later it was again strafed out, two guns being completely destroyed.

On July 7th I was posted to command in place of Major Cummins, who had been invalided home.

The following positions were occupied during the Battle of Passchendaele :—Burnt Farm (Woesten Road); Twin Cottage (Cheapside); Cactus Trench; Caesar's Nose (Pilkem Ridge).

In the middle of October the Battery pulled out and went south to the Somme area, halting en route at Arras to go into position near Tilloy Wood for a series of minor operations which lasted about ten days.

By this time the Battery had been brought up to 6-gun strength and had been awarded 3 M.Cs. (Captain C. H. Buckley, Scott, Fisher), 1 D.C.M., and 5 Military Medals.

On November 4th we went into position in Morchies, supported the Cambrai advance and retreat, and

APPENDIX

joined 90 Brigade early in December. After an enjoyable rest at Gézaincourt in January, the Morchies position was reoccupied.

At the beginning of March the Battery received its fifth and sixth guns, which added greatly to the attraction of a certain method of Fire for Effect—known in 299 as "Battery Hammer", the use of which later gave the Battery a great name amongst the infantry. It was merely "Battery Fire Half-a-second", and, to avoid accusations of plagiarism from the Field Artillery, it is admitted that the method was first adopted by them, and was originally known as "McNaughton's Hammer". It has been said that it reduced the enemy's sound-ranging instruments to impotence, and, in any case, it made a very pleasant sound and appears to have greatly impressed the infantry with the excellence of the Battery's shooting!

On March 8th the Battery was shifted out of Morchies to a position well clear of the village, where it was on March 21st, having a rear section of 2 guns near Vaulx, in charge of Scott.* The casualties sustained by the Battery during the Retreat were 8 killed and 26 wounded.

. . . .

On August 21st 2 guns of the Battery went forward on tanks with the infantry. This experiment was, in the opinion of the writer, very successful, and valuable counter-battery work was accomplished at this initial and very important stage of the final advance.

NOTE BY THE AUTHOR.—*Toc 2 and Toc 4 were each 6-gun Batteries; on March 21st each had a rear section of 2 guns on the Vaulx-Fremicourt road, but no further mention of these rear sections is made as the part they played on March 21st, though useful, was comparatively unimportant.*

TOC 5

By Major R. L. Austin, T.D., R.G.A.

Four Hundred and Eighty-Four Siege Battery R.G.A. was formed at Bordon on August 1st, 1917. I was in command from its formation. In October we went to Lydd for our shooting practice which went off extremely well although only 17 men in the Battery had previously seen war service.

We and another Battery were chosen out of 14 others to take over 6-inch Mark XIX guns: this I regarded as a great compliment as the other 12 Batteries were split up and sent out as reinforcements.

In December we went to Codford to mobilise: on January 3rd, 1918, we proceeded overseas and went into a position on the outskirts of Beugny where, after being attached to another Brigade for a few days, we joined 90 Brigade.

Do you remember how cross the Colonel was when he heard how that portable forge was stolen by some other battery from the very middle of my position one night during our first week?

By the way, I like your d——d cheek referring to that infernal Ammunition Return.*

After we left 90 Brigade in April we had rather a chequered career: at one time we served in three different Corps inside a fortnight.

Our total casualties were 2 killed and 23 wounded.

* Note by the Author.—*See page* 13.

MAJOR AUSTIN.

MAJOR CLARK.

AN UNKIND STORY

Extract from a IV Corps Order dated 20th October, 1918 :—

"*Villages will not be bombarded with heavy artillery unless it is definitely known that the civilians have been evacuated therefrom.*"

(*Scene : Toc 1's mess near Solesmes one fine morning in late October,* 1918.)

Enter Major Clark, bubbling over with joie de vivre.

" I say, Pargiter ! " said he in tones of simulated nervousness, " I've done an awful thing ! You know that big factory in E 19 ack ? Well, I was registering my guns on it an hour ago when it *suddenly* burst into flames and simply disappeared ! I hope they won't make me pay for it ! Still, not bad shooting, you know."

. . . .

Enter Major Strover an hour later.

"Good morning, Pargiter," said he, even more gloomily than usual. " My Battery did a very unlucky registration this morning. We were shooting at the factory in E 19 ack, and set it on fire. Rather unfortunate, I'm afraid."

. . . .

From the Daily Summary of the New Zealand Division :—

"At 10.45 hours this morning the Factory in E 19 a was seen to be on fire, and is still burning. It was probably destroyed by the enemy, as there was no shelling in the vicinity at the time."

H. E. W.

Roll of Officers and Warrant Officers Serving with the Brigade on March 21st, 1918.

[All R.G.A. and all Lieutenants unless otherwise described.]

BRIGADE HEADQUARTERS.

Brigade Commander	..Lieut.-Colonel A. H. THORP, D.S.O.
Adjutant	..Captain A. F. BEHREND.
Signal Officer	..A. N. GARDINER.
Orderly Officer	..R. B. BENWELL.
Medical Officer	..Captain R. VINCENT, R.A.M.C.
A.S.C. Officer	..Captain P. N. GILBANKS, A.S.C.
Regt.-Sergt.-Major	..R.S.M. J. H. OATLEY.
Artillery Clerk	..Corporal J. FULTON, M.M.

95 SIEGE BATTERY R.G.A.

Major R. B. PARGITER.
Captain A. F. STAPLETON HARRIS (Hospital, Le Tréport).
A. R. ARMSTRONG (on Leave).
C. R. BADMAN.
W. FORSYTH BROWN (on Course in France).
W. A. GRAINGER.
H. HANNABY.
J. HATCH, M.C., D.C.M., M.M.
J. A. PHILLIPS (at Ammunition Dump).
L. S. PRIESTLEY.
A. SHORE (at Ammunition Dump).
R. V. SCOTT (on Leave).
H. E. WALKER.
B.S.M. NICHOLL.
B.Q.M.S. DOYLE.

244 SIEGE BATTERY R.G.A.

Major F. LUSHINGTON (on Course in England).
Captain H. AGLIONBY.
F. B. CALLIS, M.C.
H. SCOTT GRAHAM.
D. B. MICHELL.
W. J. PASIFULL.
C. H. SMITH.
F. R. STOBBART (on Sick Leave).
G. C. STOKOE (Liaison Officer with 6th Divisional Artillery).
L. B. TIMMIS.
B.S.M. DOWLING, M.M.
B.Q.M.S. MILNE.

277 SIEGE BATTERY R.G.A.

Major R. SUNLEY, M.C.
Captain A. C. MILLS (on Course in England).
A. G. BAILEY.
W. BELL.
A. G. BENGOUGH.
D. C. DANIEL.
W. H. EDWARDS.
B. C. HARRAP.
G. C. HESKETH (on Leave).
S. WORRALL.
B.S.M. STANLEY (on Leave).
B.Q.M.S.

APPENDIX

299 SIEGE BATTERY R.G.A.

Major A. D. McKillop Clark.
Captain R. Nott.
A. W. Campbell.
F. W. Cole.
C. Farmer.
C. H. K. Fisher, M.C.
O. P. Johnston.
K. H. Rugginz.
P. White (on Sick Leave).
R. P. White.
F. W. Wild.
J. W. Scott, M.C.
B.S.M. Cutler, M.S.M.
B.Q.M.S. Trim, D.C.M.

484 SIEGE BATTERY R.G.A.

Major R. L. Austin, T.D.
Captain A. Russell (on Leave).
W. Burland.
W. P. Cook.
J. Fricker.
E. Jobling.
W. Lamb.
E. McManus.
W. Neville Penny.
E. L. O. Sachs.
M. A. Todd.
O. A. Widdowson.
B.S.M. Hughes, D.C.M.
B.Q.M.S. Freeman.

LIAISON OFFICER WITH 59 SQUADRON R.F.C.

J. D. Adamson (late 299 Siege Battery).

A.S.C. OFFICERS ATTACHED TO THE BRIGADE.

G. T. L. Macartney .. 95 Siege Battery.
H. G. Ticehurst .. 95 Siege Battery.
W. O. Duncan .. 244 Siege Battery.
C. E. Hart .. 277 Siege Battery.
H. M. Gonne .. 299 Siege Battery.
A. R. Blockley .. 484 Siege Battery.

INSTRUCTIONS AS TO THE LOCATION OF PIN-POINTS

This map is reproduced from an Artillery Fighting Map, and, in order to follow the progress of the Battle, it is essential to be able to locate the various " pin-points " referred to in the account of the fighting.

The large rectangles (lettered B, C, D, etc.) are divided into squares of 1,000 yards side, which are numbered 1, 2, 3, 4, etc.

Each of these numbered squares is considered as divided into four sub-squares of 500 yards side. These sub-squares are considered as lettered a, b, c, and d. (See Square No. 6 in each rectangle.)

The North-east of Morchies may thus be described as lying in I. 6. c.

To locate a point within a sub-square, consider the sides of the sub-square divided into tenths and find the point by taking so many tenths from West to East along the Southern side, and so many from South to North along the Western side ; the South-west corner always being taken as the origin, and the distance along the Southern side being always given by the first figure.

Thus the Location of Brigade Headquarters at Beugny is I. 15. c. 5. 5 (Rectangle I, numbered square 15, sub-square c, 5 tenths East and 5 tenths North from origin.

Similarly, the Location of the Brickfields near Bapaume. is H. 28. c. 8. 2 ; the Location of Fungus is J. 2. b. 5. 7.

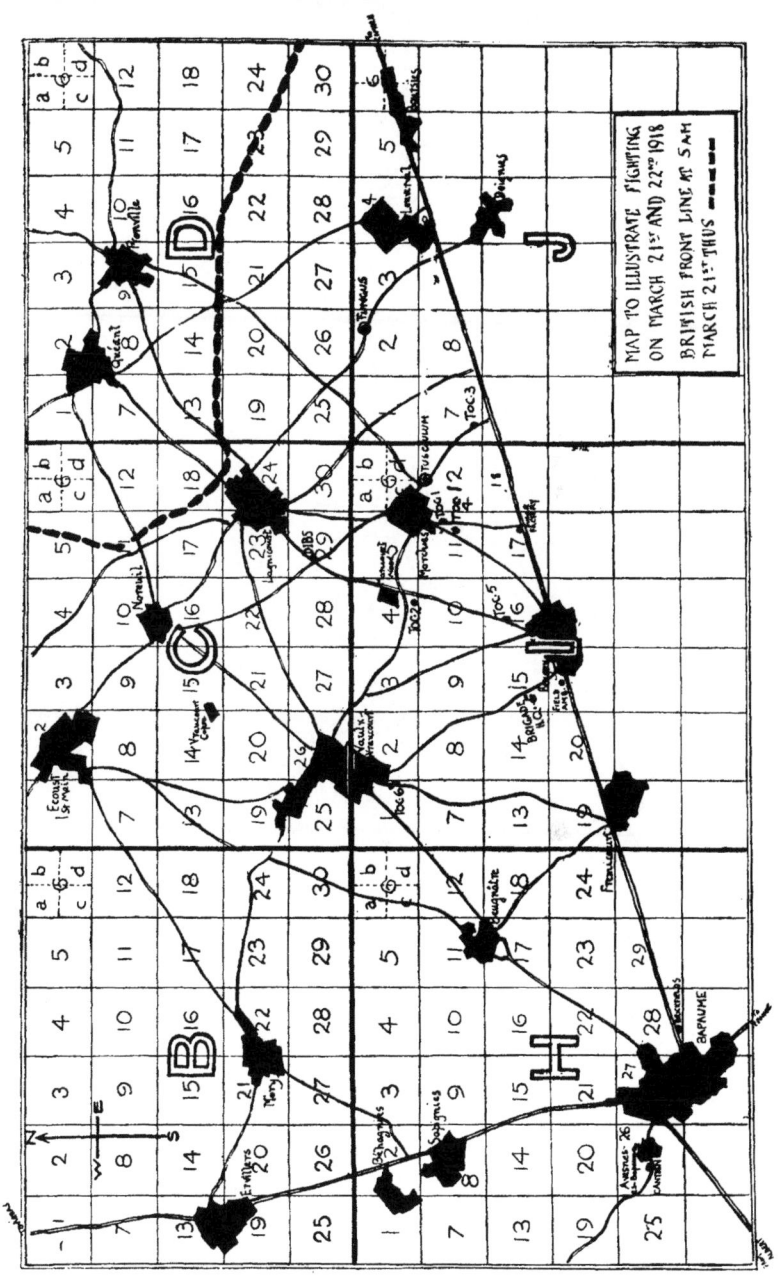

Dog, which is not marked on the map, is just south of Morchies.

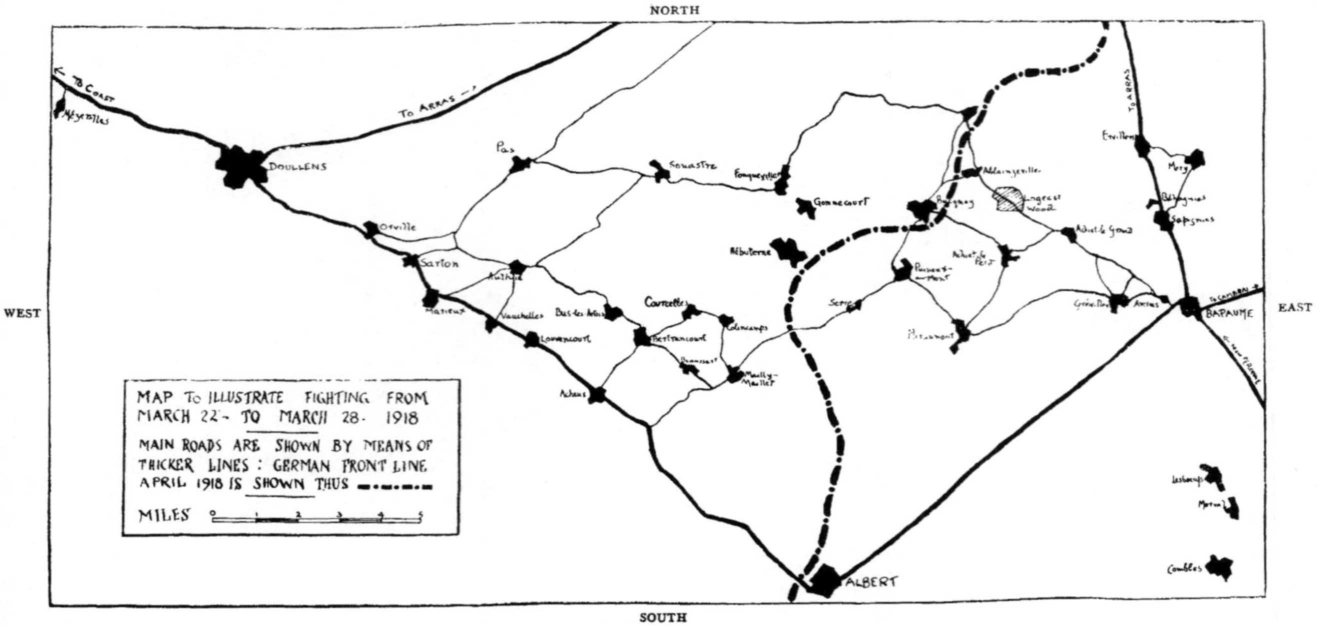
NORTH
WEST
EAST
SOUTH
TO COAST
TO ARRAS
DOULLENS
Pas
Souastre
Orville
Sarton
Authie
Bus-les-Artois
Courcelles
Bertrancourt
Colincamps
Louvencourt
Acheux
Mailly-Maillet
Gommecourt
Hébuterne
Serre
Puisieux-au-Mont
Achiet-le-Petit
Achiet-le-Grand
Ablainzevelle
Logeast Wood
Bucquoy
Ervillers
Mory
Sapignies
Bapaume
To CAMBRAI
To ARRAS
Combles
ALBERT
MAP TO ILLUSTRATE FIGHTING FROM
MARCH 22 TO MARCH 28 1918
MAIN ROADS ARE SHOWN BY MEANS OF
THICKER LINES : GERMAN FRONT LINE
APRIL 1918 IS SHOWN THUS
MILES 0 1 2 3 4 5